To Speak of God

TO SPEAK OF GOD

Theology for Beginners

URBAN T. HOLMES, III

A Crossroad Book THE SEABURY PRESS · NEW YORK

The Seabury Press
815 Second Avenue
New York, N.Y. 10017

LIBRARY OF CONGRESS CATALOGING IN PUBLICATION DATA
Holmes, Urban Tigner, 1930-
    To speak of God.

    "A Crossroad book."
    1. Theology—Methodology. I. Holmes, Janet R.,
joint author. II. Title.
BR118.H64   230   74-8917
ISBN 0-8164-1169-7

FOR JANE
Whom to be with is to be

Contents

To Speak of God

Introduction

The decision to write this book came about for a number of reasons. I hope that in having such a multiple motivation I have not failed in offering one coherent approach. For it is of great importance that persons speak of their experience of God in a single-minded manner that is both fitting and helpful. It seems that all too frequently we come away from an undoubtedly powerful and transforming encounter with the sacred only to lose its transfiguring strength in a clumsy and inept attempt to give it meaning. In these times there is a growing witness that God is present among us, and there are many examples that we are not responding to this presence in an altogether constructive way.

One example of this has been the growing charismatic or neo-Pentecostal movement. I do not question that the Holy Spirit is moving in the lives of many people who are now keenly aware of his work among us. Yet often this very experience of the Spirit is turned into cold stone by a stubborn biblical fundamentalism or a rigid moralism, which fails to see that, if God can be present now, we do not have to use the petrified representations of the past to give expression to that immediate reality. This book is written in the hope that it will free the neo-Pentecostal to express his experience so that people—such as myself—who are not a part of this movement, may appreciate what it has meant to him and share in his enthusiasm.

Another example of this growing sense of God's presence among us is to be found in the Jesus movement. I have known some young people, a few very intimately, for whom faith in Jesus has given courage and purpose to their lives. That the communities of the Jesus movement have redeemed the lives of many young drug addicts is widely known. Where our technology and our impersonal society has often been only oppressive and disheartening, the spontaneous worship and fervid sharing of the Jesus people has given meaning to many. The spirit of *Jesus Christ, Superstar* and *Godspell* has filtered down through countless city neighborhoods, small towns, and rural communities, where young people gather in the name of our Lord. Yet it seems to me that this enthusiasm is in great danger of being lost, and the old despair reinstated, unless the experience is given a substantial meaning and a balance that can last throughout a lifetime. It is to this end also that I write this book.

There are also people who have despaired of the Christian Church and have gone seeking the experience of God elsewhere. Alan Watts, the Episcopal priest turned Buddhist mystic, who died in 1973, was a pioneer in this pilgrimage away from organized Christianity after World War II. He believed that the Church had lost its nerve, had retreated into a wasteland of orthodoxy, and was unwilling to test the Spirit. I think there is truth in what Watts and countless others, studying various Far Eastern and primitive religions, have testified by their actions. Rather than depending on the sanctity of those long dead, the Church needs to risk its faith. In writing this book and in distinguishing between the experience of God and the meaning we make of that experience, I have tried to show that believing is something far more exciting than hiding in what we think is sure and certain because it is founded on the ashes of the past.

These are three areas in which people have found or are seeking the experience of God. Christian theology needs to take account of them all. The fact that many, if not most, of these people are young is why I chose to write this book with my fifteen-year-old daughter, Janet, who possesses as sharp and ruthlessly inquiring a mind as any person her age I know. On occasion she has taxed my understanding of theology to the limit by her insistence that there has to be a consistent, understandable reason for what we experience in life. I believe, therefore, that with her as a collaborator I am less likely to leave obvious gaps in my thinking and to hide the inadequacies of my argument in big words and complex sentences. Hence this book should better serve the nonprofessional theologian and lay inquirer for whom it is intended.

There are two additional motives to the writing of this book. They are rooted in a different phenomenon from the renewal of religious experience and come from my professional experience as a theological educator. They have to do with my conviction that theology needs to be taught today more as method than as substantive system.

Gabriel Moran, the noted Roman Catholic theologian and catechetical scholar, has argued that religious education must begin with adults and needs to be directed toward training them to think theologically. I agree on both counts. There is, however, very little material that approaches the question of theological method thoroughly and completely. I know of nothing that I would recommend to the educated layman who wants to make a beginning in this area. This book seeks to satisfy that need.

More specifically, I have experienced a constant frustration in seminary teaching in trying to help students "do" theology. It is all well and good to talk as we do in seminaries today of the experience-reflection-action model of learning. It is a good model, but the middle term, "reflection," is a stumbling block for many students. Our culture is not reflective, our schools and colleges do not train us to think reflectively, and we do not have a very clear understanding of what meaning is. This book is written as a primer in this area. I hope, of course, that theological students will go on to read Ray Hart, Bernard Lonergan, Karl Rahner, Schubert Ogden, Louis Dupré, and others who are writing in the field of theological method. They can begin here, however, in anticipation of going on to wrestle with the masters.

These then are five reasons why I wrote this book. It might be helpful if I now said something about my approach.

The discussion is divided into five sections, which follow logically. The first part distinguishes the difference between experience and meaning. It is only one chapter in length, but it is a crucial chapter. It is essential to the whole approach that the reader make absolutely sure he understands this difference before he proceeds.

The second part analyzes the manner in which the internal structure of meaning is constituted. There is no universally accepted terminology for those things we use to represent our experience. For some theologians "symbol" means what I mean by "sign," and vice versa. The word "myth" is very difficult to redeem from its popular and misleading use. In collaborating with me my daughter had a real struggle in seeing what was meant by a "proposition." She probably made too much of it, since I intended nothing more than a subject and its predicate.

The third part has to do with the context of meaning or the external forces in its constitution. I chose to discuss only two dimensions of this large field: community and history. Certainly there is more to the environment of meaning than these. For example, I thought of writing about the body, but a limit had to be drawn both in order to avoid making this study over long and to preserve the important principle of economy of information.

The fourth part moves from a purely methodological consideration to illustrate the approach by looking at the heart of Christian meaning. Although the illustrations in the earlier chapters are drawn from Christian sources, as one would expect of a theologian, nothing said there is exclusively Christian. In this part it is shown how Jesus, the Bible, and dogmatic and systematic theology within the Church are clearly expressions of the meaning of the experience of God as identified by a certain community, of which I and many of the readers are a part.

The fifth part is, like the first, only one chapter long. This is appropriate, since it returns to the subject matter of the first part; namely, experience as distinguished from meaning. The purpose of this concluding chapter, however, is to raise the question of how one judges the truth of one's meaning. This is to ask the question whether such a meaning accurately represents the experience in its totality, insofar as a fallible human can determine. It appears to be the obvious concluding issue. If the reader goes away feeling that I have not adequately given him a means of determining the certainty of truth, let him remember that far better men than I have struggled and continue to struggle with this issue. One can only say in the face of certain frustration, "Welcome to the human race."

It is the aim throughout to keep each chapter short. Except for an occasional further explanation there are no footnotes, and I have tried to avoid strictly technical language. In all of this the intention has been to preserve the economy of learning; that is, that the reader should carry in his mind as little unresolved or unexplained material as possible before the "pay-off." It is hoped that at every step in the way the reader can say, "Oh yes, now I see what is being said here and how it fits with what was said before."

In this regard it should be noted that theology is a discipline in abstract thinking or—as Jean Piaget, the great

Swiss psychologist, calls it—formal, operational thinking. There is no way to avoid this. According to Piaget the average person is not able to think in this way—that is, to think about thinking—until approximately the mental age of fourteen. In choosing a fifteen-year-old as a collaborator I have tried to distill the process down to its bare essentials. Even then, however, I cannot promise that what is written here will require no mental effort. It is for this reason that I have appended to the end of each chapter several review questions. This may smack of a textbook approach, but it is only meant to be helpful for those who are uncertain as to whether they are following the argument.

Furthermore, theology requires a kind of vocabulary suited to formal, operational thinking. The English psycholinguist Basil Bernstein has written that this kind of vocabulary, which he calls the "elaborated code," is not something we all possess just by virtue of being born and raised to speak the language. It is learned, perhaps as part of our native tongue or sometimes as a foreign language. I suspect that the accusation of jargon that is laid against writing in any specialized field is often only the protest of the pain of having to learn such a "foreign" language. Inevitably there will be some of this here. Perhaps the reader might approach the problem as he would a foreign language, write down the words he does not understand, and look them up in a good dictionary if they are not defined in the text.

One further general observation needs to be made about the approach of this book and about theology as a whole. Bernard Lonergan, the distinguished Canadian Roman Catholic philosophical theologian, has distinguished between "undifferentiated" and "differentiated" thinking. The former is a kind of almost instinctive or common-sense reaction to events around us, where we respond in an immediate, programmed manner. The latter is an approach to experience in which we consciously avoid the immediate response and, in order to discover the particular nuance of the experience, ask ourselves "What does it mean?" All of us are undifferentiated to a degree in our thinking; some of us entirely. Theology requires, however, the patience that goes with differentiated thinking. Often this patience appears to be a kind of skepticism or even a lack of faith. The reader needs both to avoid such a judgment and to work at developing his own differentiated thinking.

One further word needs to be said about the approach. The text is liberally larded with biblical references and quotations. This may irritate some people. The purpose is not to use the Bible as a source of "proof texts"—as is clearly evident in the chapter on the Bible. In the past, however, in both lectures and articles, I have been asked why I did not cite the Scriptures more often. I think the request is motivated by the desire to see what is being said or written as existing within and emerging from the tradition. There is a revival of interest in the Scriptures, sometimes accompanied by a regrettable literalism. My intention is for the reader to understand that what I write here is consistent with what he reads in the Bible; and that, while I reject the inerrancy of Scripture, I stand within the biblical tradition. Frequent scriptural citation should also serve to illuminate the meaning much more.

I also feel the need to add a comment about the illustrations from various Christian doctrines. Up until the fourth section the book is not specifically Christian in content, but as a Christian I use illustrations from Christian theology throughout. Those particular examples will overlap, first because I want to focus on the doctrine of God and, second, because the intended reader is not necessarily an Episcopalian, which limits my selections. I do not wish to confuse anyone for whom some of my own tradition might not be readily understandable. Therefore, it may well be noticed that I will discuss the doctrine of the Trinity in several chapters from a number of directions: the nature of Christ, the relationship of the persons of God, and the evolution of the doctrine of the Holy Spirit. It is also true that I repeatedly return to the question of the understanding of the Bible. In at least three chapters I will illustrate the material by referring to what appears to me to be a common misconception of the function of the Bible, and that stands in the way of a helpful development of theological method.

Perhaps this book sounds like hard work. Theology certainly has been that for me and continues to be. I can only share my own belief, however, that nothing is more rewarding for one's personal life. Every book I write is an exploration for me and an invitation for the reader to come along. I cannot promise what we will find along the way or that each of us will have the same reaction to new discoveries. It is a journey made in the faith that God is good and wants us to become that for which he made us. To act on such faith is to take a risk, but that is what Christianity is all about.

There are some who share in the exploration of each book without ever being asked if they wish to do so. I refer to my family, colleagues, and students. I thank them all. This particular study was conceived at the end of one period in my life as a professor at Nashotah House in Wisconsin, and it was written at the beginning of another as Dean of the School of Theology of the University of the South. Its composition has helped to make the transition easier, and let us hope that the content is enriched as a consequence.

The initial writing is mine. The revision is as much my daughter Janet's as anyone else's. My secretary, Earnest Louise Lumpkins, did a grand job of typing the final draft. Others have read the manuscript, and I owe much to them as well, particularly my colleagues Charles Winters and Taylor Stevenson. Theology, as I say in the book, is a collaborative enterprise, and this is as true for this study as for any other. I am deeply grateful for all those who have lent me their wisdom and knowledge.

Urban T. Holmes
Feast of the Holy Name, 1974

Part I

EXPERIENCE AS THE SOURCE OF MEANING

chapter ONE

The experience of God

"How can I find the words to say *what has happened* to me?" This is not an unfamiliar statement for many of us. It conveys a feeling that we all share when there is some moment of supreme joy, compelling need, or profound grief that we want to clarify for ourselves and share with others. We know the frustration even in understanding for ourselves *what has happened*, much less in telling it to others. As we begin here to inquire about speaking of God, it is very important that we think about the "something" to which we inevitably point in asking *what has happened* to me. What is that "something" that has happened?

That "something" is, in the final analysis, literally beyond words. We instinctively know this. For example, a significant number of people within Christian churches today are involved in the neo-Pentecostal or charismatic movement. This movement is well known for the presence among its members of glossolalia, or the gift of "speaking in tongues." Glossolalia has been analyzed as a kind of pre-language, a succession of meaningless sounds, that some interpret as the language of an ultimately indescribable experience, in which the participant has been lifted up to an awareness of something which cannot be captured in the images and categories of ordinary speech. It is argued that this is the experience of the Holy Spirit, which necessarily provokes a special language that is "beyond words."

In his autobiography, the English literary critic and theo-

logian C. S. Lewis told about how he got on a bus one day
not believing in God and when he got off he believed. He
could not, however, describe what happened. As he put it,
he was "surprised by joy." This was his "something"
beyond words. An absolutely indescribable thing had happened to him that lay outside of anything that he had
thought about or could achieve, and that something
changed his life.

Man exists in the midst of something-that-is-happening,
quite apart from the bits of it that we can think about and
remember in words and pictures. Life is a process or a flow
of such happenings that shapes and influences us in countless ways of which we are quite aware more often than not.
This unfolding occurrence of "happening" all about us we
may give the special name of *experience*.

The Nature of Experience

Experts in the theory of communication tell us that the
human organism is literally bombarded every second by
thousands of sense impressions of which it is never aware.
Think, if you will, of the surface of the brain as a filter
that is flooded constantly by particles of various shapes and
sizes. Only certain bits can pass through the mind's filter
to be received and acknowledged, for the purpose of the
filter is to block out all but that which the mind can handle.
My concern here is for all that goes on before anything
passes through the filter.

When I was a boy I used to love to read stories about the
early settlers in America and the Indians who were here before us. One thing that fascinated me was the accounts of
how an Indian could "read the trail," being able to tell
from the evidence that was apparent to his observing eye.
Obviously those signs were there for all to see, but only
those with special "filters" were able to grasp what was

there to be seen. What was there to be seen was experience, the presence of what happened prior to anyone noting that it happened. Experience is everything that happens, including all that no one ever notices.

Perhaps it would help the reader to think of a question such as: Did the law of gravitation exist before Isaac Newton? The law itself did not but the experience upon which he based the law did. The experience of gravitation was there, but it took a Newton to describe it. The answer illustrates the fact that the act of knowing is always open-ended. There is always more to be known, suggesting that there is an infinite world of experience that is potentially knowable.

The irony of all this is, of course, that we can only entertain the probable possibility of the existence of this experience before all awareness. The very minute we think about experience it ceases to exist prior to our thinking, and is therefore "contaminated" by our thinking. The discussion of the experience of those thousands of impressions bombarding our senses and yet still unperceived in our minds is an exercise in futility, not unlike a cat chasing its own tail. It is an attempt to do the impossible. The very nature of the situation forbids our ever capturing the object of our intentions. We are never aware of an unqualified, raw experience, which by definition is what is happening to us of which we are unaware.

This helps explain why two people never see an experience in the same way. You ask someone at the scene of a car accident, "What happened?" What he tells you in all honesty may differ markedly from what another equally sincere person standing beside him saw. We can hypothesize that the experience was the same, but just as everyone has slightly different fingerprints from everyone else, so is that mental filter unique to each person. There is absolutely no way of getting at the so-called objective truth. No person can absorb and process all the data that constitute what happened, so every experience is capable of an honest, different interpretation by man. This is what is meant when it is said that all knowledge is *subjective;* it is filtered by the self—the subject. ("Subjective" is a word, like "experience," that the reader will need to understand throughout this book.)

Some people try to reach out to acquire new data, to see within experience dimensions that everyone else appears to ignore. We speak of "blowing our minds." This is like taking a journey into a new land: Columbus sailing across the Atlantic or Armstrong landing on the moon. We trust ourselves to the unknown and let something more into our awareness, "blowing up" or "out" of our mind the preconceptions based on the data that we had been willing to allow in prior to this. It is a search, however, that only leaves us more aware of our inability to understand everything that happens.

When a young person says to his parents, "You're just old fashioned," it does not mean that a sixteen-year-old has found a different experience. The experience has been there all along. It means that he has seen the experience that he shares with his parents with different eyes. His filter is not so old (which is not to say that it is necessarily better), but it is still a filter.

I am laboring the point, which is really very simple; namely, that something is always happening of which we know only a small portion. We need to acknowledge that "something," which I have called experience and our partial and varying grasp of it. All quest for new knowledge is, tacitly or admittedly, based upon its existence; and its existence makes it impossible for anyone to claim they "know everything" or have hold of absolute, final truth. The scientist goes into his laboratory to discover something new, not on the theory that he creates that something but in hopes that through his manipulation of known data he may come to be aware of something that, although not previously known, has always been present to be experienced and known. He who claims that he knows everything that is known on a subject fails to see that something more in the experience will be perceived by another and will challenge his claim to all knowledge.

One way of defining God would be, as the exception to all this, as he in whom knowledge and experience are equivalent. As the song runs, "Nobody knows the trouble I've seen, nobody knows but Jesus"—including the singer himself. In other words, God is he in whom all that can be known (i.e., experience) is known. As St. Paul wrote, "My knowledge now is partial; then it will be whole, like God's knowledge of me" (I Cor. 13:12). Until we become as God, however, our knowledge is always inadequate to our experience.

Experience and God

Christianity is what we call a "revealed religion." It is important to understand what we mean by that, and perhaps the best way is to define "religion."

Religion is not a thing. We do not "have" religion like we have a home, a car, a bank account, or a chemistry book. Properly understood, religion is a dynamic of the person or an orientation to life. Hunger or thirst is such a dynamic or orientation. Who has ever painted a hunger or shot a thirst? Man is religious, which means that he has a need to make sense out of his life. He exists, he experiences, and he wants to know: What does it all mean? We will return in the next chapter to the question of meaning, but for the moment the important thing is to see that religion describes a *quest;* not only what Karl Marx called the opiate of the people but, more important for our purposes here, what Marx described as the sigh of the oppressed for justice.

To make sense out of life we would have to have within our grasp all of experience. We would have to know everything that is happening and be in complete command of the situation. This would require, of course, that we be without any limits in our awareness, or, as theologians would say, that we be infinite (unlimited) within ourselves rather than finite (limited). Every bit of impression made upon us would have to be processed by our minds, and we would have to have access to every particle of experience. We know this is not possible for man, and so religion "on our own" is no more than a fond hope.

God, however, does have this kind of knowledge because he is infinite. He is not limited by space and time, and the process of experience and his power of knowing are congruent. Therefore, if religion is going to be more than a cherished wish, the only possibility is for God to share with us the knowledge that makes ultimate sense of what we are experiencing. This act of sharing is what we mean by revelation. God reveals himself; he gives to us, in our longing, that universal sense of what life is all about. A religion that claims to have received such an insight is called a revealed religion.

However, revelation, like religion, is not something we "have." Revelation is the name we give to a certain kind of experience, of which we can only have a partial knowledge. The experience is that of a relationship with God, a relationship in which God intends that we become participants in a vision of life that we could not begin to attain on our own. It is God helping us to know, but still only as finite creatures with a limited (finite) capacity to know.

Perhaps the following illustration will help to make it clearer. Love is an experience much like revelation; in fact, revelation can be described as the experience of God's love. Think of the one you love. Try to tell someone what that love *means* in a way that he will *experience* that love as you do. Obviously it cannot be done. (If it could we would all run the risk of unrequited love with the wives and husbands of countless friends.) The telling (or knowing) of love and the experience of love are two unequal things; the former is only an approximation of the latter. So it is with the discussion of what revelation means and the experience of that revelation.

Revelation simply speaks of our faith in or openness to (I mean approximately the same thing by these two expressions) the experience of God coming to us to call us to a more complete knowledge. Such knowledge gives us a sense of God's understanding of life, but it is always partial, always seen as a riddle, until we are one with God.

Although some people claim to be one with God, we believe, as Christians, that only Jesus had this relationship. It can be argued that in his historical form Jesus "emptied himself" (Phil. 2:7) of the knowledge that comes from such oneness to share truly in man's limited nature. So while we can claim that we all share in the experience of God, no one can equate what we say about that experience with the experience itself.

This point is very important for the rest of this book, and unless the reader grasps what is being said he will miss the import of everything that follows. In the last section of this chapter I will make concrete some of its implications in an intentionally controversial manner, challenging the reader to explore the meaning of the distinction between the experience of revelation (interpersonal meeting between God and man) and the knowledge (description of that experience) that one may claim to have of God's vision of creation and our life within it.

Illustrations

In the following three illustrations the reader should note the *difference* between what we make of an experience in terms of a description and the experience of God to which it points. The former is always relative to the latter, and we cannot claim for it the absolute quality that we believe the actual experience of God to possess.

First of all, many people speak of the Bible as the *Word* of God. This is inaccurate and can easily lead to the conclusion that the word of God is reducible to the Hebrew, Greek, Latin, or English language. The Bible is in fact a record of the Christian community's experience at different times in history of the word of God. We can speak of it as inspired; that is, as an authoritative source for the correct understanding of that experience. But there is much in the experience of God that is not found in the Bible. As the fourth evangelist wrote: "There were indeed many other signs that Jesus performed in the presence of his disciples, which are not recorded in this book" (Jn. 20:30).

In fact, the term "word" itself is deceptive. It does not refer simply to the sounds or letters that stand for something, but to the whole notion of an ordered, rational cosmos manifested in the gift of speech and in the process of knowing. The principle meaning of "Word" is then the revelation of God, the experience of God's vision, which makes sense of life. If we fail to see the distinction between that and the human words of the Scriptures, we miss a very important point and fall into the error of fundamentalism (literal, word-for-word claim for the inspiration of Scripture), which no amount of reverence for the Bible can overcome. (The role of the Bible will be the subject of the entire ninth chapter.)

A second illustration is seen in the error of identifying one ecclesiastical institution or group as *the* true Church, as if it understood the entire experience of God in Christ. Claims of absolute truth require that we know everything that is to be known in God's coming to man; or—which amounts to the same thing—that we are convinced that nothing can be uncovered in that experience which would contradict what we hold. There is a certain comfort in such certainty but it cannot stand up under examination. It fails to understand the many elements in our condition that shape the filter through which we perceive the experience of God, no matter how good our intentions or how dramatic our sense of God's presence in our lives.

We often identify this attitude with the Roman Catholic Church, but there is also a tendency for certain groups outside that august institution to take on the air of having a direct pipe line to God. Occasionally a charismatic group will fall into this error. The point is that "pipe lines" are all limited and cannot carry infinite messages. I will develop the meaning of this point further in a later chapter, but for now the reader needs to separate the experience from the expression.

Finally, in the field of ethics there can be no claim to possessing a law that covers every possible situation. If there is such a thing as divine or natural law, we do not know such a law. We have only human laws. They can attempt to guide us in our experience of life, but they are partial because they are human. There is always the exception, which not only tests or tries the law, but in fact shows that it is relative to the total experience.

For example, is there no situation in which killing another human being might be right? Those persons today arguing *for* abortion and euthanasia are often the same people *against* capital punishment and war, and *vice-versa*. In neither position can we find an absolutist case against taking a human life. Then again, is it not the wedding alone that lifts sexual intercourse from vice to virtue? There are many sexual relationships having the benefit of license and priest that are utterly sinful. Is there no occasion in which stealing is not the better thing to do, given the situation? Certainly the principle of private property does not prevail over the saving of a person starving from hunger. The courts of our land have struggled for years to find a law to cover "obscenity" and failed. Law is a most important institution, but it is never equal to its task of guiding us in the proper course in all experience. We cannot account for all experience.

Summary

The reader is perhaps saying to himself by now, "Yes, yes, I understand. Why not get on with it?" Let us make sure, however, that we grasp the essential point. It is so easy for this difficult distinction to slip away between what we claim to know and what we can only point to (the experience from which we have drawn our knowledge, which is much greater than our knowledge). When we do this our theology tends to become identified with the mind of God; we make idols of our opinions and judge others as if we knew as God knows.

It is better that we maintain a more humble, a more human stance, and hold that while we believe that we do experience God, we have no absolute claim upon that experience. When we seek to make sense of it, we are always influenced and distorted by our human condition. The truth of our knowledge of God depends on a whole process, which I shall outline in the rest of this book. We begin, however, with the experience that is ineffable, unutterable, and inexpressible. It is an experience common to all men, for God loves all men and wishes to make himself known to them; but we are all limited in our own particular ways as to what that experience can mean.

The story is told of Thomas Aquinas, one of the greatest of all Christian philosophers, that toward the end of his life he experienced God in a most dramatic manner. Of that experience he is reputed to have said, "It makes all that I have thought, said, and written mere straw." It works the other way, as well. If we have the experience of God and attempt to say, as we must, what it means, we need to begin by acknowledging that our words will be only "straw" before the glory of God's presence itself.

REVIEW QUESTIONS

1. *Why is it that once you think about an experience it ceases to be an unqualified, raw experience, and something else is added?*
2. *What does it mean to say that revelation is an interpersonal, subjective experience of God, in which he seeks to give us knowledge that we cannot otherwise have?*
3. *Why is it impossible for anyone to have a "direct pipe line to God," and why does this mean that the Bible, the Church, and the law are all a step removed from being God's Word?*

Part II

THE INTERNAL STRUCTURE OF MEANING

chapter TWO

The meaning of God

For several years I taught a class in preaching in which one of the requirements of the students was that they deliver a sermon at a regular Sunday service, which sermon would be criticized following that service by a committee of lay persons. The preacher was not to be present and the criticism was to be taped. I remember one particular response to such a sermon, which was prototypical of many of the post-sermon discussions. The gathered group were asked to discuss the question: What did the preacher say to you? This particular sermon was on the second coming of Jesus. One man answered that the preacher had said to him that America was a great country and that God was with us. A younger person, perhaps about eighteen, said that she heard the sermon to say that if we did not "get right with God" soon that the whole country was going to be taken over by the communists. A third person reported that for her the preacher said that there was no reason to fear death, that God would take care of her when she died.

This is, of course, an illustration of the not very unusual multiplication of meanings in hearing a sermon, which reminds us that while experiences may be identical, it is their *meaning* that we have to go on. By *meaning* we should understand *the terms in which we hold the experience in our minds, interpret it, and use it for a basis of action.*

Meaning, then, is what a person makes out of an experience. It is the answer to the question: What does it mean?

Meaning is drawn out of experience, although it is never equal to the experience, as we have seen. Meaning leads to action. We can only intend to do that which is available to us in our meaning. You cannot prepare for the second coming of Jesus if you live in a world where it makes no sense to think of someone returning to earth after an absence of almost two thousand years. Man differs from the other animals in that he has the capacity to act out of meaning instead of simply responding to a stimulus—such as the wink of an eye, the jerk of a leg, the withdrawal of the hand from the fire.

My own use of meaning is not, however, set over against animal experience, as would be the case in a narrow, rationalistic, or conceptual notion of meaning. I see meaning as related to and growing out of that part which man shares with all of life. The ability to give meaning to experience is, in this sense, something that has been developed to an increasingly refined art through the evolution of life. Man's capabilities are the highest expression to date of his ability to work within meaning, but it emerges from his animal history.

Meaning takes on a number of dimensions, one of which we may have in common with other animals. This will be discussed in the next section as "felt" meaning. The important thing is to see it as a product of the person's attempt to make sense out of life in some manner, clumsy or precise. This is the meaning that exists within our awareness and stands for the experience. When our experience is challenged, it is this meaning with which we oppose the threat. When we are asked to share our experience, it is this meaning—and only this—that we can consciously offer.

The Gospel is the meaning of God as drawn out of the Christian experience. But keep in mind what we have already said: such "good news," as far as man possesses it, is always partial, always shaped by what we are in time and space, and is only an approximation of the God who reveals himself in Christ. Furthermore, within this partial grasp of experience, there are four dimensions of meaning which will constitute the outline of this chapter.

Felt Meaning

Try this exercise for a minute. Answer the question as best you can: What am I? You are asking, of course, what does it mean to experience me? Make a list, mentally or on paper. When you run out of descriptive words—male, white, American, student, eighteen—ask yourself if this exhausts what you mean to yourself. The chances are very good—almost certain—that there is something more. Look deeper. Look at yourself in a mirror and ponder your feelings about yourself: love, fear, hatred, anger. Probe deeper and try to get into touch with those things that shape your whole orientation to the world around you, as well as to yourself. You find that this list is not exhaustive either but consists of a collection of feelings that recede into a kind of murky obscurity.

My experience is that the deeper I probe into the question of what I am, the less precise becomes my understanding but the stronger are my feelings. The undergirding notion of my experience of myself consists of powerful images whose origin lies buried in my past. These images are inevitably seen as defining a relationship of ourselves to other persons, and most touch upon a profound sense of dependence, acceptance, love, or compassion. Yet there is also a sense of gazing into the unknown, the void that is not penetrated by our own knowledge, a sense that confronts us with the ultimately mysterious quality of life itself.

This meaning is basically a feeling because we all live in

this world in terms of our bodies. We can and do move beyond our bodies, but we begin by understanding ourselves and others (including God himself) through our embodied existence. Recently a psychoanalyst, Robert Lifton, suggested that man is born with certain obscure images of meaning within his mind, including a sense of life beyond death. Because this is true, I emphasized in the beginning of this chapter that man's ability to give meaning to his experience is rooted in his animal evolution. As I shall mention in a later chapter, this is what the coming of the Christ, called the Incarnation (embodiment), is all about.

The meaning of our experience begins then with our feelings. What does not awaken our emotions is generally of only passing interest to us at best. Our feelings are like sensitive tentacles, gathering data worthy of our further mental exploration. Put another way, we can say that any experience of which we become aware is first translated into felt meaning before it becomes important to us.

Why does the astrophysicist explore the meaning of the stars? I suggest it is because he is seized by the wonder and immensity of the heavens. Why does a medical researcher seek for the cure of cancer? Undoubtedly because he is moved by the suffering caused by this dread disease. Why does the civil engineer spend long hours designing new structures? I suspect it is related to the thrill of creation. In the same way, the experience of God first engages us in feeling. No one comes to believe as a result of playing games with words or pondering some theory.

Some years ago I participated in a survey of adult confirmands in my diocese, where we sought to find out what brought them to the Episcopal Church. The overwhelming response was that either attendance at a service or a relationship with another Episcopalian had lead them to this point, both of which were essentially encounters of feeling. I would go so far as to say that the church service or the significant Christian person gave them a "handle" on those murky feelings of dependence or love of which I wrote before. This delightful sense of the mysterious which we understand as the presence of God, was given a form sufficiently specific that it could be interpreted into action—in this instance, becoming an Episcopalian.

Religious meaning always begins with feeling. John Wesley, the founder of Methodism, recalls that the pivotal moment of his ministry was at the meeting at Aldersgate in London when he felt his heart "strangely warmed." The great sixteenth-century Spanish mystic, Teresa of Avila, describes her most intimate experience of Christ in terms not unlike a sexual orgasm. As one theologian has put it: "Faith is the eyes of love." Such feeling is not to be identified simply with a fleeting emotion, but it does possess a strong visceral or "gutsy" quality that is a key to the fact that felt meaning is the most powerful meaning. We are seized and compelled to action by felt meanings. Many who are part of the charismatic movement today know of what I speak. Meaning without feeling is sterile and lifeless.

The problem with felt meaning is that it lacks clarity and precision. Without further refinement it can beget all kinds of action. There are people who as a result of a religious experience have engaged in sexual orgies, slaughtered masses of people, left families to starve, or have condoned bribery and false witness. In an age such as our own, when a large number of people have experienced what we call emotional "highs," which constitute a religious felt meaning, it is very important that we recognize this danger, so that we can do justice to their experience without creating a mindless, chaotic reaction in the Church that will repel many.

The refinement of felt meaning can move in one of two

directions: common-sense meaning, which is a conservative (meaning "to conserve") response; or intuitive meaning, which is an innovative response (as in having a "hunch").

Common-sense Meaning

An airplane was flying over the Rocky Mountains with a great number of passengers. Suddenly one of the engines caught fire, then another one went. There was great panic in the cabin, and someone screamed: "We're all going to die, someone pray!" There was a dead silence. Then he cried out again: "Well, if no one can pray, for God's sake do something religious." So they did. They took up a collection.

This anecdote defines common-sense meaning and reveals its problems. Common sense is what everyone knows. It is the ingrained assumptions of a society that are accepted without much question. I was brought up in a world in which black people were known by everyone to be bearers of disease, to be irresponsible and lazy, and to be incapable of intelligent behavior. No one questioned it that I can recall. We had strong feelings, just like those people in the doomed airplane, and we let our felt meaning be interpreted by what the society as a whole assumed. Everyone knew that black people were "just that way"; just as everyone knows that what you do when you want to be religious is pray and take up a collection.

This kind of unexamined assumption can be anything from foolish, as in the case of the anecdote, or grossly immoral, as in the matter of prejudice against blacks. It is the result of letting one's feelings be refined by the notions *conserved* within the society. The problem is that we turn over our responsibility for what we feel to the community as a whole, without asking whether the society's response is just or appropriate or whether it more accurately reflects the broken and sinful nature of this world.

Obviously, much of our meaning has to be common sense. We are brought up to live in a particular kind of community and appropriate action here has to become second nature for us. If you have ever moved from one part of the world to another you will know what is meant by "culture shock." I recall once being transferred from the south Louisiana swamps to the Wisconsin woods. The very problem of adjusting and of finding the patterns of living I had taken for granted in one place and that generally did not work in the other left me depressed for a year. Culture shock is a symptom of common-sense meaning and the fact that what is common sense for one place is not for another. We overcome culture shock by developing the habits of the new place (becoming acculturated).

Let me emphasize again the absolute necessity of such common-sense meaning. We cannot think through for ourselves the meaning of every experience. We would be utterly frustrated in our attempts to process all that happens to us. At the same time, however, we must recognize that the world changes, and legitimate common-sense understanding of experience for one period can hang on for a hundred years till it ceases to represent the experience accurately or—even worse—embodies not the word of God, but the devil's work.

We have an illustration of this in nineteenth-century revivalism, which spoke only of individual responsibility before God, and dwelt heavily upon our guilt by appealing to vivid images of hell as compared to a heaven somewhere "off there." It operated out of an authoritarian and fundamentalist view of the Bible. Such a view is no longer used in America to open man to the *freedom* of Christ. On the contrary, it has become an accomplice of the repressive.

sinister elements in our society. The name of this God of latter-day Puritanism is invoked by those who avoid the issues of justice, liberty, and equality; *and yet it has the power of appealing to America's common-sense religious meaning.* The matter is very subtle, and the stakes are extremely high. I will honor the reader's perspicacity or ability to judge acutely and only call his attention to the proclivity of government to wrap itself in the mantle of common-sense religious meaning. The effect is often destructive of the experience which the meaning once represented; to wit: the liberation of the person and the reconciliation of the nations.

Intuitive Meaning

The alternative to the conservative approach is the innovative, which is the source of intuitive meaning. It is possible that when a person draws from his experience a deeply felt meaning, instead of understanding it in terms of the common-sense meaning of the society, he seeks to discover new implications for that experience and to shape novel ideas. Often this can be a community function, which will be the subject of the sixth chapter.

The Wright brothers, for example, working in their bicycle shop, believed passionately that man could fly in a heavier-than-air craft. They tinkered, played with hunches, experimented, until in 1903 at Kitty Hawk, North Carolina, their imagination bore fruit. Thomas Kuhn in a study called *The Structure of Scientific Revolutions* has pointed out that scientific breakthroughs are the result of a pressure building up between scientific axioms (the common sense of scientists) and the data of experience until some intuitive person constructs a new theory to explain the unexplained experience.

If we think of the history of Christian theology, we will

see that it is an intuitive struggle by the Church to explain an experience that no previous categories could encompass. You could say that the formula for the nature of Christ defined at the Council of Chalcedon (451), which said that our Lord was one person in whom two natures, divine and human, was the culmination of the kind of encounter first recorded in the Fourth Gospel. There a man cured of his blindness by Jesus was examined by the Pharisees as to who Jesus is. The man replied, "What an extraordinary thing! Here is a man who has opened my eyes, yet you do not know where he comes from! . . . If that man has not come from God he could have done nothing" (Jn. 9: 30, 33). The Pharisees expelled him for his intuitive reply, which conflicted with their common sense.

We do not hold the imagination in very high regard in our society. This is certainly ironic. It was imagination that sent Columbus out across the unknown deep to discover the New World. It was the imagination of the first English settlers that brought them to our shores. It was the imagination of Jefferson and his colleagues that framed the Declaration of Independence. We are prone to dismiss the novelty of intuitive meaning by saying, "He's only imagining it." The hope for the future lies in such intuitive thinking.

This is risky, of course, because it requires that we be strong enough to take the chance of failure. Imagination requires a secure person, not afraid of ridicule or of being proven wrong. The man who prefers to stay at home and play it safe will feel very uncomfortable with intuitive meaning. Like the Pharisees all through the Gospels, he will stick to common sense. Part of the danger in intuitive thinking is, quite frankly, that it becomes more than imagination; it becomes fantasy. The difference between imagination and fantasy is that the former is a playing with possibilities in a manner that follows as reasonable from our past meaning. Fantasy is discontinuous with the past. For a scientist to propose moon flights on the basis of rocket technology developed by the Germans in World War II is imaginative; but for me to suggest that we build a time machine to transport us all back to 1776 because I saw such a contraption in a TV show is fantastic.

Thinking Meaning

The criteria against which we measure the distortions of common-sense meaning and the possibility of fantasy in intuitive meaning lie within "thinking" meaning. When I write about thinking, I intend the word in a narrow sense, of which "ratiocination" or "cognition" are synonyms. I shall also use "reason" or "reasoning" in the same sense. It means precise or logical thought, closely reasoned and exact. Our feelings can fool us and bring us to common-sense or intuitive meanings that can range from silly to destructive. For an obvious example: insisting on the literal interpretation of Jonah and the great fish is silly; handling poisonous snakes as part of a worship ritual is destructive. Both positions fail when we think reasonably about them.

There are other illustrations of this principle which are more subtle. This presents us with a particular problem, therefore, because in America's history there is a virulent anti-intellectualism that has recently taken on a new life in the churches as a result of a resurgent experimental religion. For example, several years ago members of the "Jesus movement" interrupted a talk by the Lutheran theologian Dr. Martin Marty in Berkeley, California, to insist that he stop talking about theology and discuss "real religion." The tragedy of such anti-intellectualism is that it makes us victims of our feelings, as mediated by common-sense or intuitive meaning or directly. We could end up supporting the bombing of helpless people in the name of Jesus or confusing a psychotic break with a call from God.

Thinking meaning is never enough by itself, but it is an essential element within the four dimensions of meaning. It is a response to the question: Is it true? Our answer comes when we construct some conceptual description of the experience and test it against that experience. (A "concept" is the result of thinking.) If we judge that such conceptual insight does in fact meet the conditions of the experience—the experience as shared by all—then we can consider it true until further conflicting data is encountered.

An appropriate illustration of this might come from the Creation story. Archbishop Ussher of Ireland in the eighteenth century dated the age of the earth as approximately six thousand years. He did this by means of a chronological calculation using the genealogies in the Bible. Few questioned him then because there was no data to stimulate a widespread refutation. Today, on the basis of such scientific data as fossil remains, clear indications of the necessity of a slow evolution of life, astrophysical calculations, and carbon 14 dating, we know the earth to be anywhere from two to ten billion years old. There may be disagreements about details, but no one who examines the data of our present experience of the earth's history can agree with the Tennessee legislature, which recently passed a law saying that the literal interpretation of Genesis is deserving of equal consideration with the hypothesis that the earth and its life evolved over billions of years. To interpret the Genesis story as an historical account is not an acceptable thinking meaning in the face of our present experience because it cannot account for most of the conditions of that experience. This account does have great value as myth, as we shall see.

Thinking meaning gives clarity and precision to our experience. It becomes a means of shaping well-defined action and of sharing our understanding with others. The danger is that thinking meaning, by itself, is sterile and cannot evoke a strong response. It does not charge the imagination and it can convey such unpalatable truth that the community will reject it out of hand. If it is to provide us with a balanced understanding of experience and provoke us to action, it has to combine itself with felt meaning.

Summary

Meaning is what we make of experience in terms of our feelings, what society tells us, our hunches, and our reason. The following chart shows how we move from felt meaning to common-sense or intuitive meaning and on to thinking meaning, yet need to maintain a balance of them all.

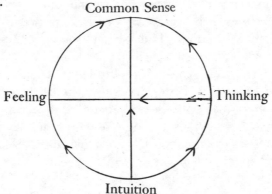

One further word is in order. If I paint a picture, write a book, carry on a conversation, sing a song, build a house, do a job, or perform a ritual, it is all meaning: picture, book, conversation, song, house, job, ritual. As soon as we move from the unexpressed experience to make something of that experience, we are involved in meaning. The result of this book, therefore, is concerned with how we construct the meaning of God. We have made the distinction between experience and meaning, and now we are going to talk about the latter. It is important, of course, that we never forget that no matter what we do with the meaning of God, not the Bible, the sacraments, the Christian confessions (e.g., the Westminster or Augsburg Confessions), the papal decrees, or our image of Jesus himself is the *last* word.

REVIEW QUESTIONS

1. *What is the difference between experience and meaning?*
2. *Meaning begins with what? In what two directions does it generally move?*
3. *What is the importance of thinking meaning in relation to all other forms of meaning?*

chapter THREE

Symbols and ritual

We began with the experience of God, moved to the meaning of God, and now we leap to symbols and ritual. Much of American religion is heir to an opinion, as old as the sixteenth century, that the Christian Gospel is free of superstition and clear in its import. It has sought to maintain this outlook during a persistent, if not altogether consistent, attack from the intellectual world over the past two hundred years. We Christians are not to be confused with ignorant savages, working their magic and pleasing angry gods by their sacrifices. The German martyr of World War II, Dietrich Bonhoeffer, said that Christianity is not a "religion," which would suggest that it operates at a level above the "symbols" and "rituals" of paganism. This is an outlook which, I would surmise, may be shared by persons of simple Christian commitment who have never heard of Bonhoeffer, who never had to defend their belief against the intellectuals, and who know nothing of the sixteenth century.

We are speaking of meaning, however, and the construction of meaning is like the building of a house. Man has always experienced a need to avoid cold and wet weather, and for this end he has constructed shelter. Anthropologists have discovered remains of the dwellings of man's ancestors hundreds of thousands of years old, built out of sticks and stones. These were the materials available, and were appropriate to his life-style. The forms of shelter since then have been more complex, as they were expressive of the history and environment of man. The Eskimo builds an igloo, the Indian of the great plains a tepee, the early settler of the forests of our eastern coast a log cabin, the medieval baron a stone tower (which we call a "castle")—and I live in a sophisticated home of brick veneer. The life-style of the people and the available materials in the area dictate the composition of the response to man's experiential need for shelter.

Shelter in all its forms is a meaning appropriate to one experience; religious meaning is a product coming out of another experience, an experience of God. Yet religious meaning, like shelter, is constructed from the material available in our environment according to our life-style at that time in history. Our way of doing things and the images we find ready for building such meaning change, but they are always of two kinds: *signs*, which I will discuss in the next chapter; and *symbols*, which together with signs make up the *representations* that constitute religious meaning.* Representations are the bricks, the stone, the lumber, the concrete, from which we build religious meaning. No such meaning can be considered whole—perhaps none can even exist—without both symbols and signs. Therefore, for reasons that shall become obvious, symbols and rituals are essential to the Christian experience and its meaning.

The Nature of a Symbol

There is a tribe in Central America who worship their "high god" under the form of a spider. This may seem primitive or gross to us. Remember, however, that religious meaning is constituted from the environment and life-style

---

* My use of these terms is based on the work of the theologian Paul Tillich and is somewhat different from that of other scholars. For the benefit of the reader with a further interest in this topic, there is an Appendix at the end of this section on "Representations and Their Synonyms."

of the people who experience the divine. The pagan Romans of the first and second centuries found it revolting that Christians drank the blood and ate the flesh of their Lord. They considered them cannibals. We may laugh at their misunderstanding, but perhaps we grasp the meaning of the early Christians just as inadequately as did the pagan Romans by "spiritualizing" the symbol of the Eucharistic presence of Christ. In other words, perhaps the ancient Fathers of the Church intended a more material notion of Christ's presence in the symbols of bread and wine than we think.

What is a symbol? A symbol is a representation of an experience and points to something or some relationship within that experience. It also does something more; it provides us with *a means of participating in that something or that relationship*, which otherwise could not happen. The Holy Eucharist is such a symbol. (Perhaps the reader thinks of it more as a sacrament, but for my purposes here a sacrament is a symbol to which the Church has given special authority.) As symbol the Holy Eucharist enables us to participate in the experience of Christ's death and resurrection in the fourfold action of taking the bread and wine, blessing it, breaking the bread, and eating and drinking the elements. We cannot be present in any immediate manner at this event, which occurred almost two thousand years ago, but the power of that event can be mediated to us by such a symbol.

This means that a symbol possesses power. Recently an Episcopal priest of evangelical persuasion challenged my talk of symbols and asked me: Where is "the saving power of God" (Rom. 1:16) in all this? He missed the point. Here in the symbol is the saving power! It engages us first of all at the level of *felt* meaning. As I have already said, the most powerful meaning is that which we feel. The beginning of all religion is in the area of feeling, the feeling of dependence, love, awe. For this reason we can begin to see that the root of religious meaning is the symbolic. But let us first consider further the nature of symbolic power.

One of my colleagues at the University of the South illustrates the power of symbols by describing an incident which occurred to him while teaching a class in liturgics (the science of corporate worship). He had there an ex-master sergeant who found the whole course a bore. The sergeant was a Vietnam veteran, a no-nonsense American who prided himself on being a very practical, hard-nosed man. The class discussion was on symbols, and it was very obvious from the sergeant's expression that he was simply not interested. "Do you know what a symbol is?" my colleague asked him. "No," the sergeant replied. "Why should I?" So the instructor took an American flag from the corner and began to lower it to the ground. The sergeant suddenly came alive and was obviously anxious. "What would you do," my friend asked, "if I would drop this flag and spit on it?" The sergeant replied, red with anger, "You damn Commie, I'd knock your head off!" The instructor paused and then said quietly, "Sergeant, this flag is a symbol for you. Look at its power to make you angry."

The power of the symbol is like a magnet; it draws us deeper into the experience it represents, pulling us into the unknown. The core of God's self-revelation is perceived by us as symbolic, for it solicits us to become the person God has created, but who is as yet known only to God. Again, recall that I said that religion begins with a *feeling* of God's presence—a feeling of being called to something more. Someone may protest that it is not a symbol that calls us, but the real thing—God's word. Nothing is more real in our meaning of God, however, than the symbol.

The nature of this magnetic power may well be attributed to the fact that symbols are always a bit incongruous, ambiguous, or imprecise. Marshall McLuhan, a Canadian scholar who has written a great deal on the effects of contemporary communication media, describes what he calls "cool media." Cool media are those forms of communication that engage more than one of our senses (television, for example, involves sight and sound), and are partially implicit in their message. That is to say, there are gaps in the material communicated, which the receiver fills in automatically. Consequently, he is drawn into participation. Symbols are something like cool media. They characterize what the psychologist Jerome Bruner calls "thinking with the left hand." A symbol is not used logically, it does not carry a one-for-one representation of a thing or a relationship in experience, it is the language of analogy or metaphor. "God is a loving Father" is an analogy or metaphor. We know that God is not our biological father, nor is he charged with the responsibility of rearing us. Rather he is *like* the best possible father we can imagine. Since there are some of us for whom fathers are never a good thing, we know that sometimes all analogies fail. Another analogy would be the comparison of religious meaning and shelter with which I began this chapter.

What I am saying is that symbols possess several possible denotations at once, and also carry many connotations. A denotation is an explicit referent. For example, the water of Baptism *denotes* life, cleansing, and birth from the womb. Water is involved in all of these. Water also can connote, however, in some dimly understood manner, the ancient seas from which all life sprang, or the watery habitat which at least one anthropologist suggests was the abode of early man not so many millions of years ago.

Symbols are also capable of evoking a variety of emotions at the same time, sometimes even conflicting emotions. When Moses was out in the wilderness tending his father-in-law's sheep, he saw the "burning bush" from which God spoke. He was both fascinated and afraid (Ex. 3:1-6). If you have ever had the misfortune to come upon a very bad highway accident, you know the feeling. There is the desire to stop and look, accompanied by the horror of seeing the blood and pain of another human being.

Two examples of this multiplicity of feeling, which bear remarkable resemblance to one another, might help the reader understand my meaning. The first is from Teresa of Avila's description of the experience of God she calls "rapture," a deeply symbolic encounter with Jesus.

In these raptures the soul seems no longer to animate the body, and thus the natural heat of the body is felt to be sensibly diminished; it becomes gradually colder, though conscious of the great sweetness and delight . . . it comes like a strong, swift impulse . . . you see and feel this cloud, or this powerful eagle, rising and bearing you up with it on its wings . . . though rapture brings you delight, the weakness of our nature at first makes us afraid of it.

Teresa wrote four hundred years ago and is considered a "Doctor of the Church" (i.e., one of its great teachers). This next passage is from the most recent book of a contemporary American anthropologist, Carlos Castaneda, and describes a religious experience he had, with a coyote as the principal symbol.

The coyote stood up and our eyes met. I stared fixedly into them. I felt they were pulling me and suddenly the animal became iridescent; it began to glow . . . the coyote was a fluid, liquid, luminous being. Its luminosity was dazzling. I wanted to cover my eyes with hands to protect them. The luminous being touched me in some undefined part of myself and my body experienced such an exquisite warmth and well-being. . . . Suddenly I felt that my body had been struck and then it became enveloped by something that kindled me.

In both of these passages there is a flood of different kinds of feelings, often moving toward conflict.

The magnetic power of the symbol is in its ambiguity. ("Ambiguity," meaning that something has an uncertain, obscure, or double meaning, is an important word to remember.) The varied emotional impact caused by ambiguity can be understood further if we realize that the symbol protrudes only partially into our consciousness and seems to operate at the edge of our awareness. As the proverbial iceberg, only a small portion of the symbolic meaning is visible, and when we surrender to its power we are led out beyond our previous knowing. An example of this is the sexual symbol. The reason why I would oppose the trivial approach of such magazines as *Playboy*, *Penthouse*, and *Gallery* is that their glib exploitation of sexual feeling obscures the full significance of what is in fact a mystery that leads to God, the mystery of the most intimate of interpersonal relations. The sexual symbol properly seen as such is inexhaustible.

It is also very risky, which is indicative of an important dimension of symbolic representations of experience. The less explicit our meaning, the more we operate in uncertainty. The sexual symbol, for example, requires a certain surrender of the self to the other. We do not stay in control, we have to trust to their love. For this reason, we can be genuinely afraid of what the other will do to us. This is why sexuality is surrounded for many by a rigid moralism, impotence, excessive prudishness, or at least a retreat from honesty about sexual feelings. I am surprised to notice this sometimes in persons who claim to have a deep commitment to God, as if God made a mistake in creating us as sexual beings.

This discussion of the nature of a symbol should lead us to the conclusion that the heart of religious meaning is the symbolic representations that lie within our environment. You can work at an assembly line without symbols, which is part of the problem of such work. You cannot give meaning to the experience of God, however, without symbols. It is tragic that today some persons who honestly want to know God try to find him without symbols. The risk is too great for them. Instead they settle for "canned meaning" by idolizing old dogmas or misusing the Bible. This is particularly regrettable among those who speak of the experience of the Holy Spirit and then try to explain what it means by a mindless biblical fundamentalism or a leap backward into seventeenth-century dogmatism. It contradicts the whole notion that the Spirit sets us free and brings us to maturity in Christ.

The Nature of Ritual

The regular, patterned source of symbolic meaning is ritual or liturgy. A ritual or a rite is a bundle of symbols. If symbols are necessary to religion, so are rituals, for they give structure to the particular symbolic experience of the religious community. The purpose of a ritual is to evoke the feeling of the primary experience that a community holds as essential to the knowledge of God, and therefore to draw the participants into the power of that event.

For Christianity that event is the coming of Jesus Christ, and particularly his death and resurrection. Therefore, the Eucharist is the rite containing those symbols that evoke the experience of Christ's dying and rising again. It is to this function of the symbol that Luke's Gospel points when Jesus says of the Eucharist: "Do this as a memorial of me" (Lk. 22:19), "memorial" meaning *make present again*. It is to this purpose that Paul refers when he says of the Eucharist, "For every time you eat this bread and drink the cup, you proclaim the death of the Lord, until he comes" (I Cor. 11:26).

In our country people often dismiss ritual as silly or unimportant. Strange as it seems, this is even true of persons who claim to be very religious. I used to have a college professor who insisted that the Church service be absolutely devoid of ritual, but oddly enough he was the state Grand Master of the Masons, an organization given to elaborate ceremonial. Ritual has a way of catching us. Undoubtedly, certain liturgies can be sterile and the power of their symbols obscured, but ritual will have its way. Have you ever considered how a country like the United States, which rejected kings and the pomp surrounding them, has bestowed upon the Presidency a ceremonial as complex as that possessed by any monarch?

The spirit of American nineteenth-century revivalism has traditionally rejected the ancient liturgies of Catholic Christianity: vestments, music, art, architecture, color, and movement. Yet today this same spirit has produced the rather gauche extravaganzas such as went on in Dallas, Texas, in 1972 as "Expo '72"; and in London, England, in 1973, as "Spree '73." Often this kind of ritual is an attempt to find symbols that can be controlled in order to avoid the risk of deep symbolic meaning. The result is a parody of the real thing, and such ritual has no sustaining power, no ability to reach us with God's love at the heart of our bafflement, suffering, and evil.

At this point it should be obvious that a life without ritual, formal as well as informal, is an empty life. The Eucharist is a formal ritual; the manner in which someone returns from work and enters his home is an informal ritual. A life without ritual is likely to be barren of powerful meaning. This barrenness is an accusation leveled at America by some very wise persons who note our obsession with technology and the fact that as a people we play down the importance of ritual. The reason it is essential that persons participate regularly in religious ritual, which for me means the liturgy of the Church, is that without it they starve. They starve for lack of "symbol-feeding," which enables them to build a meaning of the experience of God. They starve because without such meaning they cannot feel, imagine, or think that life has any real sense to it.

The reader must not make the mistake of thinking that a quiet moment at the edge of a lake or the reading of a book can be substituted for regular participation in the ritual of a religious community. Rituals and their symbols have an integral relationship to the *corporate life* of all of us. The sense of God's presence is the gift of the community, and not something the individual possesses merely by virtue of his inner reflection. We do not make symbols on our own, we find them. Ritual is the most important place in which to find them.

The Source of Symbols

Rituals can be private, they can belong to a particular society, or they can be the common property of man. Perhaps the religious person of the greatest attraction to us (a symbolic or sacramental person) is one whose private symbols have a way of engaging our public symbols.

When I was five years old I visited Europe with my family, and one of the few memories I carry of that time was standing in a little room in Edinburgh Castle in Scotland where James I was born in the sixteenth century. There is a legend that his mother, Mary Queen of Scots, lowered him in a basket out of a little window in that room, down the side of a cliff, in order that he might be baptized as a Roman Catholic. I long carried the memory of looking out that window while my oldest sister told me the story. Recently I returned to Edinburgh Castle and stood again in that little room and looked out that window. I was transported back in time, with all the feelings that would accompany such an experience. This is an example of a private symbol. If this can engage a symbol we share—such as a special place associated with someone we love—perhaps I and my private symbol have a certain power for you.

At the funeral of the Christian martyr Martin Luther King, his body was borne through the streets of Atlanta, Georgia, on an old wagon drawn by a mule. To someone from Europe this conveyance of the body may have seemed quaint, but nothing more. To someone like myself, brought up in the South, familiar with the oppression of the blacks, in which I had a part and against which King lived and died, this was a moving sight. It is an example of a societal symbol.

I have already mentioned the symbols of the common meal found in the Eucharist, sexuality of which there are only hints in the Bible (Ephesians 5:25-33), and the waters of Baptism. I might add here that the waters of Baptism also relate to death and birth, burial and emergence. As a people we do not have much immediate experience of death and birth, but when we do we come to know the mystery of life that is known there. It is a mystery which has always moved man in powerful ways. These symbols then—the meal, sexuality, and death and birth—transcend any given society and culture and are part of the heritage of all mankind as he has evolved out of the distant past. They are examples of universal symbols.

Obviously a religious meaning has greater applicability and power when its symbols are universal instead of societal or private. The truth to which it witnesses has longer life as well when its symbols are not merely the property of one person, a small group, or even a single society. For the meaning will not die when that person, group, or society dies. Therefore, the source of the symbols we use, be it in our rituals or outside this regular pattern, is very important for the source of our meaning.

Summary

We have been discussing the construction of religious meaning, the "stuff" with which we seek to make sense of the experience of God. Of the two kinds of representations, this chapter has been devoted to symbols, their nature, their use in ritual, and their source. I have argued that the basis of all religious meaning—that is to say its power to evoke feeling that is primary in such meaning—is the symbolic. This is why ritual, which is nothing other than a bundle of symbols, lies at the heart of religion. It is also why we should carefully consider the source of our symbols.

The nature of a symbol is a slippery thing for many of us. Symbols are the most important part of meaning to us all, because they lie at the heart of our reality—they are the most "real" thing we know! (For example, someone we love, who is a symbol for us, is more "real" than the 1040 form on which we file our federal income tax.) Therefore, it is very important not to let the definition slip away. A symbol has many references, explicit and implicit, which makes it possess ambiguity. It engages us first at the level of feeling, and these feelings are often varied and perhaps conflicting. A symbol is an analogy or metaphor, stimulating our intuition or imagination. A symbol is not something we make, it is something we discover.

So much for symbols for the moment. The other kind of

representations are signs, to which we now appropriately move.

REVIEW QUESTIONS

1. *What are the two categories of representations that make up the internal structure of meaning?*
2. *What is a symbol and what is its relationship to ritual?*
3. *What is it that makes a symbol possess a magnetic power, the ability to solicit man into spiritual growth?*

chapter FOUR

Signs and propositions

Symbolic meaning is not the result of our efforts. It is not something we produce by trying hard. Symbols emerge in our consciousness by means of the very opposite process, by letting go, by opening our thoughts, or by "blowing our minds." This is even true in terms of our private symbols, such as my experience of standing in the small room in Edinburgh Castle, looking out the window down the steep cliff. A minute before walking into that room I had no thoughts of *producing* the powerful wave of feeling—love for my family, the bittersweet sense of a childhood lost in the past, the delight in history—that overwhelmed me for those brief moments. The symbolic meaning *found* me, if you will, even though the nature of my trip made me open to this. The same is true, for example, when we participate in the Eucharist. We do not *make* Christ present by much speaking or elaborate ritual. He finds us there, if we are open in faith. Often this involves a patient waiting.

That meaning, usually common sense and thinking meaning which we do produce by our own efforts, is related to signs and propositions. (What I mean by "proposition" will be defined at length later.) Anyone who has labored hard over a mathematical equation or sought to describe in the best English prose the events of the American Revolution or attempted to prepare a program to be fed into a computer knows what demanding work these things are. They require clear thinking, precision, logical argument, and a vocabulary that accurately represents its referents. This is the language of signs and those combinations of signs we call propositions. This book is written largely in signs and propositions, although I hope that the illustrations may find you on a symbolic level to give power to my meaning.*

Meaning that is made up of signs *only* is, for reasons we shall see, very sterile and dull. Therefore, some religious enthusiasts are against too much propositional meaning. In some ways I can sympathize with them. They want feeling in their faith, and if we are constantly reducing everything to a logical system they feel deprived, and rightly so. Thus are the seeds sown for an anti-intellectualism in religious meaning. In an effort to preserve the emotional component in belief, we can overreact and reject all efforts to understand in clear and precise terms what that belief means.

This anti-intellectualism can be more than a mistaken reduction of religious meaning to feeling only. It can also be the disguise for a way of looking at the world that is destructive, self-serving, or just plain "sick." All strong feeling is not from the experience of God, even though we choose to label it that way. This is one way of interpreting St. Paul, when he writes, "Satan himself masquerades as an angel of light" (II Cor. 11:14). The father of psychoanalysis, Sigmund Freud, was not entirely wrong when he claimed religion was an illusion or the projection of a wish, grounded in our own inability to live responsibly. Reason and its use of logical signs can be a means of exposing such perverted religious meaning, and the results can be painful. We all resist such pain, and consequently we can act against the instruments of an honest evaluation of our beliefs.

If I say that religious feelings must stand the honest scru-

* Again, the reader who has a particular interest in my use of these terms is referred to the Appendix at the end of this section.

tiny of logical evaluation, I am not suggesting that all our heartfelt belief is ultimately an illusion. I am saying that signs, and the propositions composed of signs, are part of that total meaning we construct from experience. Just as the foundations of religious meaning are symbols, so the superstructure and its refinements consist of signs.

The Nature of a Sign

Let us, therefore, take a closer look at the nature of a sign.

The symbol was, as we saw in the last chapter, ambigious, analogical, and powerful. The sign is quite different. It is clear, precise, and carries as much as possible a defined one-to-one relationship to its referent. In other words, that to which it points is unambiguously seen in the single denotation carried by the sign. H_2O is, without question, the chemical formula for water, not carbon dioxide. The humerus refers to the bone in the upper part of the arm or forelimb, and is not to be confused with the femoral or thigh bone. A paronym is a word that has the same derivation as another word, and is not a synonym. As a matter of fact, the value of these formulas and words lies in their ability to define clearly a thing or the relationship of things, which makes them extremely valuable tools in the development of a logical system. At the same time they carry very little excitement with them—they have small symbolic value.

We need to keep in mind that the word "logical" comes from the Greek word *logos*, the same word that appears in the opening verses of the Fourth Gospel, where it is declared that the "Word (*logos*) became flesh." The "word" here is not simply the combination of sounds that we represent on a page—the Greeks had another word for that (*rēma*)—but represents the belief that behind the language of signs there lies an ultimate or cosmic order of reason. What the evangelist is saying is that Christ is the supreme expression of the *divine logic of creation*. For man to seek to understand the experience of God in terms of the tools of reason or logical thought—that is, by signs—is completely appropriate. As a matter of fact, such rational understanding has been viewed by some as the very heart of a spiritual experience.

A sign, as I have already implied, only points to its referent. It is not a means of participating in it. What it gains in precision and clarity it may well lose in power and magnetic pull. Signs dominate in common-sense and thinking meaning, just as symbols are primarily operative in felt and intuitive meaning. When someone seeks to "explain" their feelings or "make concrete" their intuitions, they move to the sign language of common sense or thought.

An example of this is our Lord's question of his disciples, recorded by Matthew, "Who do men say that the Son of Man is?" The disciples had a feeling or intuitive reaction to Jesus, but what are they to make of that? Some of them replied with common-sense signs, according to the tradition of the Jewish people: John the Baptist, resurrected from the grave; Elijah, whose return just before the dawning of the Messianic Age was traditionally anticipated; Jeremiah, the prophet of the Exile reborn; or the "Prophet" the Book of Deuteronomy had promised as a "new Moses" (Deut. 18:15-22). It was Peter, whom Jesus praised, who had apparently pondered that question very deeply and who offered a somewhat more thinking meaning: "You are the Messiah, the Son of the living God" (Mt. 16:13-16). The point here is that they all experienced Jesus, they all possessed positive feelings (or they would not be his disciples), and some "explained" their feelings in terms of the more readily available and safer common-sense meanings. Peter was more thoughtful, went "out on a limb" and called him the "Christ," the anointed one. Most of us now avoid thinking and use common-sense answers to the question, "Who do you say I am?"

There is a certain additional "something" in the story of Peter's confession that we need to notice carefully in passing. Peter's affirmation of who Jesus is possesses a quality that is more than a simple theological definition. It has greater symbolic power to turn men's hearts than, say, the formula propounded at the Council of Chalcedon, where Jesus was said to possess two natures, one divine and the other human, in one hypostasis or person. Yet Peter's confession is a theological concept, just as the Chalcedonian definition is. In this way we see illustrated the fact that signs can have symbolic power as well as signative quality.

The nature and possibility of the power of a sign depends upon a variety of situations. Peter's response to Jesus affects us because it is a "breakthrough" in the midst of growing tension over the person of Jesus and his acceptance by the Jews. The setting gives it power. Words by themselves, however, irrespective of their immediate context, can have the quality of both symbol and sign. Words are made up of sounds, and certain sounds evoke special feelings. Compare your response, for example, to words like tomb, womb, dead, and lead to words like bright, light, quite, fight, and tight. They all have different denotations, but the connotations of the first set have a common feeling which is quite different from the feeling evoked by the second set. Scholars who do research in the emotional impact of sounds have isolated certain vowels and diphthongs that are related to specific kinds of felt meaning. Preachers and teachers particularly need to keep this fact in mind, but so do we all when others respond with very strong feeling to certain words and propositions we use.

Propositions and Truth

A proposition is a combination of two or more signs in which there is a subject and predicate (a sentence). The predicate is a verb, sometimes with the addition of a noun or adjective that relates to the subject. For example, "God is love" is a proposition with a subject (God) and a predicate, consisting of a verb and an adjective (is love). "God loves" is a similar proposition, as is "God is a lover," but the former employs only a verb and the latter a verb and a noun. We are using very simple propositions to explain this, but the more complicated forms are nonetheless built about this basic use of subject and predicate signs. (Every time the term "proposition" is used in this book I intend the thing defined in this paragraph. Before proceeding the reader needs to be sure he understands.)

Having defined what a proposition is, we may identify three kinds of propositions. It is very important to keep the function of each of these three clear in our mind when using them to build the meaning of the experience of God.

The first kind states a point of view. This can be an ethical statement ("Abortion is wrong."), an outlook on the world ("God is the creator of the universe."), a personal report on feelings ("I love you."), and so forth. We use such statements all the time, and they have meaning to those who share the point of view expressed there and to those who understand the referents of the signs but do not agree.

It must be recognized, however, that it is very difficult to prove the truth or falsity of such statements. For example, a debate is raging throughout the United States today over whether or not abortion is wrong, and ultimately the question is resolved upon the consensus of feeling with which we identify. Another example would be the fact that, as the author of I John 4:12 points out, God is not a part of our immediate experience (no one has ever seen God), so there is no way of testing the claim that he is the creator of the universe. Still a third example is that of love, which is a very ambiguous emotion that cannot be separated out and measured in such a way that there is no question as to the truth or falsity of my claim to love someone. In fact, many statements of points of view are circular in nature. This means that the predicate is contained in the subject and the statement could be reversed and it would make no difference. An example: "The creator of the universe is God."

Some years ago Paul van Buren, a theologian now teaching at Temple University, suggested that statements about God were meaningless because in our society the word "God" referred to nothing in contemporary man's experience. Van Buren undoubtedly overstated his case, but the point he made does illustrate the fact that statements of points of view, if they are to make any sense, must have an agreed "something" in a community's experience to which the subject refers, even if it is only a shared feeling or outlook. It follows that such statements are often meaningless to other communities where this referent is not identifiable in their experience. For example, Exodus 22:18 says that all witches shall be put to death. As a contemporary command this is meaningless to me, since I live in a culture that does not experience "witches," even though I can understand that other people at another time may believe they have experienced them.

A second kind of proposition is that which claims to add information on the basis of possible verification—that is, testing its truth or falsehood—either by direct observation or by citing recognized authority. For example, if I said, "All Episcopalians are white," I would be claiming to give my hearers some information. It could be tested for its truth by examining all Episcopalians to see if indeed they were white. Again, if I said, "Thomas Jefferson wrote the Declaration of Independence," the information could be tested by various methods; by comparing the handwriting of the original with a sample authentically known to be his, by reading what those present at the time recorded, or by comparing the style and ideas of the document with those Jefferson expressed elsewhere.

These kinds of statements are based on the observation of data. The predicate does not necessarily follow from the subject but is attached to it because of what someone claims we can perceive in our experience. Some people would claim that no propositions about God (no religious meaning) can be of this kind, because God is not an object of our experience. Others would agree with the claim that God *himself* is not an object of our experience, but would counter that it is possible to discern *indications* of God, such as order and creativity, which we can attribute to God. We can, they say, make statements about these indications and consequently state informational propositions about the meaning of the experience of God.

The third kind of proposition we might call one that awakens us to some new insight. These are called disclosure statements, and are a means of creating a new consciousness in us. Sometimes we hear something said that is meaningless to us for a long while, and then, suddenly, we "see the light." This is a disclosure statement. A great deal of poetry is of this kind. Usually disclosure statements have a strong feeling attached to them and form a metaphor. For example, I was once struggling with telling a twelve-year-old boy about heaven in order that he might find it a desirable goal. It suddenly struck me that I had seen him out of my office window walking over to the church carrying a football. I said, "Heaven is the best possible football game played forever!" "Oh," he replied, "I see. It must be great!"

My equation of heaven to football is a metaphor. Some of the most important things said about God are metaphors. "Jesus is Lord," "Our Father who is in heaven," "The Word was God." Football games, lords, fathers (important men upon whom we depend), philosophical notions of the Word, or reason are all things we experience in this life, qualify to an infinite degree, and then attribute to God. We know that he is much more than these things, but we are trying to evoke a sense of what the experience of God is like, admitting that this only points in the right direction.

Building Propositional Meaning

When we use signs as subjects and predicates, as well as various means of qualifying subjects and predicates, shaping them into propositions, it is important that we do not use one kind of proposition as if it is supposed to do something for which it does not have the ability. If we understand this we can save ourselves much frustration.

For example, recently I was in a hotel in a strange city on Sunday morning, having just returned from an early service. For the sake of something to do I turned on the television and watched in amazement the preaching of a local pastor, which was in a style utterly foreign to me. One sentence of his sermon, delivered with much anger, I recall vividly. "In this church here," he bellowed, holding up his Bible, "we don't have any atheistic, intellectual, evolutionary, communist snobs!" The implication was that if you were one of these horrible things, you were all of them. Since I would plead guilty to holding to the theory of evolution and since I consider myself an intellectual by trade, I thought that perhaps I might also be a snob, but I am neither an atheist nor a communist. Then I asked myself, Why do people sit there in rapt attention, as the choir behind him seemed to be, and listen to that nonsense? As I think about it, of course, the answer is that this proposition is not one that he intends for me to prove, and it is not even meant to convert me (it is not a "disclosure statement"). It simply states a point of view that he shares with his audience and wants to reinforce for his and their comfort and reassurance. This realization is all the more frightening since there is no way of breaking into this kind of vicious, destructive thinking by proof or insight!

We all are subject to this kind of statement. I heard the editor of a very liberal journal describing all conservatives as "unthinking," "fascist," and "selfish." That is her point of view. We can only judge its value in terms of our own hierarchy of values: forgiveness, love, reconciliation, fairness. Most religious conversation we hear and use is of this kind. I suspect that it is the least productive kind of propositional meaning, but because it is so common, we need to recognize it and see it for what it is.

What we need more of is propositional meaning that awakens us to God's presence among us and clarifies the indications of his presence that we can discern in our world. This is to say we need religious poetry, story, and metaphor. We need to work at a philosophy of ultimate reality, which is called "metaphysics." The word "metaphysics" is derived from the Greek philosopher Aristotle, whose discussion of ultimate questions came *after* his analysis of the natural order—"meta" (after) and "physics" (nature). Both disclosure propositions and those subject to verification are the hardest kind to make, because they require either an acute sensitivity to intuitive meaning (as in Chapter Two) or a very keen perception of logic. Not everyone can possess this brilliance, and if they do not, they should be careful not to expect or claim too much for what use they do make of signs and propositions.

Summary

In this chapter and the last one we have discussed the materials with which we build the meaning of the experience of God. Symbols dominate in the felt and intuitive realm, and signs in the common-sense and cognitive dimensions of meaning. We have now outlined the appropriate capacity of each, symbol and sign, and their operative form, ritual and proposition. This has been to speak of the *internal* structure of meaning, and it will be necessary to turn to the context in which such meaning is constructed: community and history. But first it is essential that we devote some space to a certain "mixed breed" of the structure of religious meaning, which uses signs and propositions to weave a symbolic narrative: *myth.*

REVIEW QUESTIONS

1. *What is the nature of a sign? Of a proposition?*
2. *How does a sign differ from a symbol? What value does a sign have that a symbol does not have?*
3. *There are three kinds of propositions discussed in this chapter. What are they and why is it important to be able to distinguish religious discourse in which each is used?*

chapter FIVE

Myth

A myth is a true story about God and man. Most people think of myth in exactly the opposite sense. "It's only a myth," we say, meaning that it is a figment of our fantasy life, something we thought up that is quite untrue. We talk about the Greek myths of gods sitting on Mount Olympus, eating ambrosia and dabbling in the affairs of man. We know that God does not work this way and therefore such stories are myths. In thinking this way we lose a very important insight into religion and ourselves.

A myth, as I suggested at the conclusion of the last chapter, is a symbolic narrative. It tells in story form a truth which we could not otherwise grasp or experience. Notice that this is the definition of a symbol—something which represents that which we could not otherwise know and in which we can only participate by virtue of the symbol (baptismal waters as a representation of and means of participating in the death and resurrection of Christ). This is why I describe a myth as a symbolic narrative. *It makes no difference whether or not a myth is historically true.* By historically true we usually mean that if we had been there we could verify the account by taking pictures. Such a point of view would argue that the resurrection of Christ is historically true, because if we had been there on Easter morning we could have made movies of Jesus being raised. The understanding of myth as something apart from historical truth saves us, on the one hand, from asserting the historicity of what our reason tells us cannot be so, or on the other hand, from feeling compelled by reason to repudiate a story that has a great deal of power in our lives. We do not have to be caught in the logical trap awaiting those who insist on the absolute, literal historicity of everything in the Bible. The religious journalist Lester Kinsolving illustrates the point in describing the obvious impossibilities in certain Old Testament myths. For example, in regard to the story of Jonah, a very important didactic tale, literalists are unable to answer the question, "How was Jonah able to breathe while inside the belly of that great fish for three days"? Concerning the powerful Judaeo-Christian myth of Adam and Eve, they cannot explain that if Adam and Eve didn't know the difference between right and wrong—in fact were so dangerously ignorant that they weren't even aware of their nudity (Genesis 3:11)—how could they reasonably be blamed for eating of the Tree of Knowledge?

It does no good to get angry or explain it all as a mystery. Certainly God is a mystery. This means, however, that no account can *reduce* God to human events which leave him in inevitable contradictions. The understanding of myth as any story, historical or imaginative, which relates a truth that is above event, is what gets us out of this dilemma. The contradictions, therefore, belong to the myth and not to God. The contradictions produce the ambiguity which is what points with power to the God who is indeed mysterious.

More on the Nature of Myth

Many fields of study speak of myth: religion, anthropology, literature, philosophy, natural science. My interest here is to discuss myth in an anthropological and theological sense, without doing violence to the understanding of other disciplines. My goal is to help the reader see the importance of myths in our life and religious meaning, and to acknowledge this importance gladly.

First, myths are necessary for humans. All men seek to make sense out of their existence. This is what we have described as the religious drive, and that "making sense" inevitably takes a story form. Ritual, the heart of religion, is often an *acting out* of myth. The great Christian myth is the death and resurrection of Christ (which is also an historical event), and the Eucharist acts this out in a somewhat hidden manner. Symbols are embedded in the ritual and its myth (bread and wine, Body and Blood, altar and people, the Kiss of Peace). However, the symbolic narrative—that is, the myth—gives the basic understanding of the ritual, which may blossom into thinking meaning or systematic theology. Not all religion, however, has theology, and some people suggest Christians ought to avoid theology and simply live their myths.

Perhaps another illustration of the relation of ritual to myth will help clarify the universal nature of myth, as well as its function in the significant rites of our life. The celebration of Christmas began with a festival established in A.D. 336 by the Roman Emperor Constantine to counter the great feast in the most significant revival of Christianity of that day, Mithraism. The original intention was to emphasize the teaching of the Incarnation, the Word made flesh, but we have come to think of it in terms of the nativity story in Matthew and Luke. This account of Joseph and Mary going down to Bethlehem, the birth in the stable, the announcement to the shepherds in the fields, and the coming of the Magi is a legend, which draws its power from a myth. Speaking for myself, I doubt its historicity, but the story is very important to me. The family and parish rituals it affects and explains are a vital part of my life. Such a myth is as important to me as the myth of the coming classless society is to a communist.

A second point is that myths are contextual, cultural, and communal. Like symbols, myths are not invented, they evolve out of the history of a people. I mentioned the nativity story. I question if you had been standing on a street corner in Bethlehem in the spring of 6 B.C. that you would have seen a carpenter from Nazareth, Joseph, and his pregnant wife, Mary, being turned away at some inn.* One reason I believe this is that the story itself bears close relationship to other accounts of the birth of divine persons, going way back into man's dim history. The narrative in Luke and Matthew, particularly with the highly metaphorical account of the three wise men or astrologers (anticipating the acceptance of Christ by the non-Jews), stands in a very important and revered mythic tradition. This myth was not the invention of the authors, but rather the result of their use of a whole tradition to say something about the experience of Christ. I might add, however, contrary to my own position, that possibly God, knowing the tradition, could have so shaped the historical event of Christ's birth in order to fulfill it.

Because myths are communal, some people would call a story like Jonah a pseudo myth, because it appears to be a contrived, literary composition. Such a story is quite different from the early chapters of Genesis, which partake of a whole tradition. I personally consider Jonah, with its images of death in the waters of chaos, and resurrection after three days in the belly of the great fish, as well as the preaching of repentance as the condition of reconciliation

---

* 6 B.C. is the best possible date for Jesus' birth, taking the description of Luke as an actual event, for example, the census of Quirinius, the shepherds in the field.

with the living God, a recounting of some very important timeless themes. It bears obvious relation to Christian Baptism. It is true, however, that no one can think up out of "whole cloth" their own personal myth any more than he can make his own personal symbols.

It follows from all this, in the third place, that our myths are what shape our view of the world. In this way a myth is like a proposition that defines a point of view, but it does it with much more power and subtle effect. The reader will recall the television preacher in the last chapter and his vehement denunciation of "atheistic, intellectual, evolutionary, communist snobs." What he is saying is very much like what I heard a Tennessee radio preacher say. Our problem in America, he explained, is that we no longer believe in the devil. And he went on to comment: "The devil doesn't wear a red suit and carry a pitchfork. The devil appears under all kinds of disguises. He teaches in our colleges, he's the long-haired 'hippie' liberal down the street, and he writes in our newspapers defaming our President."

The radio preacher gives a bit more explicit illustration of the myth that lies behind the first preacher and his enrapt congregation. It is helpful to look into this myth to see how, like all myths, it shapes a world view. Unless I am very wrong, it is based on the image of the cosmos as divided between two forces: God and the devil. The devil is winning because, as they can see, all the things they hold dear are threatened on every side. Therefore, they feel hard pressed, which produces a chronic paranoia. "The devil, like a roaring lion, prowls around looking for someone to devour" (I Peter 5:8). Their only hope is to hold fast to Jesus, who takes on the color of what makes them feel good: such as football, America first, individualism, white supremacy, material prosperity. People who do not like football, who suggest America is not always right, who live in communes, or who are poor or black, are very suspect. The devil is in them and God does not like them.

It happens that this is a myth in which I do not share. The important point at the moment is not to debate this, however, but to see that the myth shapes the viewpoint of the people who hold it. In fact it is so pervasive that when we encounter people who do not share our myth we often judge them to be either evil, stupid, or insane.

The effect of judging others because they do not share our myths leads to a fourth point, namely, that myths order our behavior because they order our world. They present to us the options of good and evil, and they become the guideposts by which we educate our children. Take, for example, the American myth of "manifest destiny." This is the name for the conviction that it is the obvious will of God that the United States rule from Atlantic to Pacific. It motivated the Louisiana Purchase, the annexation of the Republic of Texas, the taking-over of California after the Mexican-American War, and the slogan "54-40 or Fight" that led to the acquisition of the Pacific Northwest, not to mention the purchase of Alaska. Perhaps the myth of "manifest destiny" was not too bad until it led to the imperialist attitude toward Latin America, the involvement in such wars as the Spanish-American and the recent Vietnam conflict, summed up in a foreign policy that begot the "ugly American."

The fact that myths do order our behavior, sometimes in a tragic manner as in the case of recent American history, makes it most important that we be aware of the operant myths in our lives. They are universally present in all of us, they are the product of the community to which we commit ourselves, they shape our world view, and consequently they are the basis of our actions. Myths themselves, however, are no more than stories—although true—by which we interpret our experience, and one that is destructive can be replaced by one that is in accord with our highest values. This is not always easy, however.

Choosing Your Myth

One great value, among others, of education is that it greatly increases our options. If we lived in some isolated culture, untouched by other peoples and living amid very slow development, we would find that there would probably be one dominant, homogeneous myth, interpreting our experience of God. There would be little choice in world view and consequent behavior. There are societies today, where the authorities seek to produce this situation artificially. The communications systems are isolated from others and the population is saturated with a single party line. Such information control has as its purpose the elimination of choice of myth, which effectively controls motivation and behavior. The agony of the Russian novelist, Alexander Solzhenitsyn, and the fact that the manuscript of his latest novel, *The Gulag Archipelago*, had to be smuggled out of Russia and published abroad, is a case in point. Of course, the very opposite of information control is what we want.

In the spirit of education, Herbert Richardson, a theologian teaching at the University of Toronto, has written about three basic myths of transcendence in religion. The first is the separation-and-return story. This story encourages the notion that the individual is nothing in himself, and only when he gets back to "mother earth" does he recover his identity. The image is of man's *unhappy* expulsion from the mother's womb—as in the story of the Garden of Eden (Genesis 3:8-24)—and the search for a return, which is satisfied only in the tomb. The similar feeling between the words "womb" and "tomb" is not accidental. This myth is characteristic of primitive religion, but it is also found in those contemporary Americans who blame all our problems on technology and seek to "return to nature." This is sometimes called "Post-Ruskinism," after John Ruskin, a nineteenth-century architect who despised industry and advocated a return to an agrarian society. The present youth cult of the American Indian, which Robert Bellah, the distinguished American sociologist, calls the "paleolithic revival," the agricultural communes, and the popularity of organic foods are symptomatic expressions of this myth.

A second myth is much better known in the traditional American understanding of Christianity. It is that of conflict-and-vindication. In this story a person is not someone in himself, but acquires his identity (salvation) by conquering the enemy (the devil, communists, organized crime). The basic motif of the "western" novel or movie, ending with the "shoot-out" where the "white-hat" guns down the "black-hat," is a perfect expression of this myth. Conflict-and-vindication lies behind both the television preacher and the radio preacher I described previously.

It is interesting that the hero in this myth, the "saved Christian," ultimately comes off as a dull, faceless, pious, "plaster saint." The interesting person in this myth is the personification of evil. The contrast between Satan in Milton's *Paradise Lost* and the Christ in his *Paradise Regained* is a very good illustration of the point. When we understand this I think we have a clue as to why American Puritan Christianity appeals largely to persons whose lives are unbearable or who are simply afraid to death.

The third fundamental myth of transcendence in Richardson's scheme is that of integrity-and-transformation. Examples of it can be found in early Eastern Christian tradition, which developed quite apart from the Western obsession over the conflict with sin. It has taken on a new life in contemporary society with the notion of higher consciousness, self-authentication, and personal awareness. A current advertisement for perfume, both on television and in the press, is a good example of this myth. It shows a modishly dressed young man, with a similarly dressed, "sexy" blonde leaning on his shoulder, discussing being your honest self. The ad ends with her saying, "If you want him to be more of a man, try being more of a woman." The implication is that life becomes what we hope it might be by each of us "getting ourselves together," integrating our identity or role.

Various psychologists (Abraham Maslow, Gordon Alport, Carl Jung, Erik Erikson) have led the way in recalling us to this myth but the myth itself is certainly subject to a Christian interpretation. The problem is that the past fifteen hundred years of Western Christianity (western Europe and America) has seen little exploration of its possibilities. Yet it is worth thinking about, and the reader might reflect on what it means to be adopted as a "son of God" (Gal. 4:5), to have "the mind of Christ" (I Cor. 2:16), to "for a short while be lower than the angels" (Heb. 2:7). It occurs to me that this describes a movement of growth, as the Eastern Church (Greek, Russian) has said, from mortality to immortality. We do not trade in an old, corrupt nature for a new, saved nature. Rather the nature with which we are born matures and takes on anew the strength for which it has the potential.

Summary

The purpose of this chapter has been twofold. The obvious intent is to introduce the reader to a phenomenon within religious meaning that is not simply reducible to symbol or sign, felt and intuitive meaning, or common sense and thinking meaning. We need to become aware of the nature of myth, which is a propositional narrative that carries a symbolic power and purpose and is interwoven with ritual, the heart of religion. (A "propositional narrative," of which this book is an example, is a series of propositions, whose purpose is to describe, explain, or tell a story.)

We come now to the conclusion of this part of the study concerned with the internal structure of religious meaning. It is important for the reader to be sensitive to the subtlety of myth as it leads him to make a certain kind of construction of religious meaning, and to be careful that he is not captured in one kind of myth. There are options, and we need to explore them in all their manifold forms. The value of what we have drawn from Richardson's threefold analysis is that he identifies certain basic types, of which many myths are an elaboration. This enables us to discover that at different points in history certain decisions have been unconsciously made within communities to follow this or that basic type, and if we are to overturn what has become the destructive results of certain myths, we need to go back to basics.

This brings us now to two very important chapters, developing two themes in the construction of religious meaning, themes often misunderstood if grasped at all. This is the context of that construction: our *community* and our *history*. Keep in mind that religious meaning is what we make of the experience of God, and those materials from which we build that meaning can only come from our environment, which includes our body and our community, and our history or past. We are not isolated minds operating in a vacuum. We are our community and our past.

REVIEW QUESTIONS

1. *What do we mean when we say that a myth is a true story or a narrative symbol?*
2. *What are the four functions of myth outlined in this chapter? How do they relate to the reader's understanding of his personal myths?*
3. *What is the effect of each of the three myths outlined by Richardson? Where does the reader's dominant personal myth fit?*

appendix

Representations
and their synonyms

This appended note is *not* necessary for an understanding
of this book. It is intended for the occasional student, who
may speculate as to how my use of "representations,"
"symbols," and "signs" corresponds to similar terms for the
internal construction of meaning. Therefore, I will provide
a very brief summary of some possible relationships.

The word "symbol" comes from the Greek, *sym-ballō*,
combining the root for "to throw" or "put" with the suffix
meaning "together." In my use it is always positive or
creative. I realize that in the quest for the symbolic it is
usually true that we encounter images that become destructive. I do not discuss these in this book, but I do
reserve for them the name "diabols," from the Greek *dia-
ballō*, combining the same root for "to throw" or "put"
with the suffix meaning "apart." A diabol is the opposite of
a symbol, and relates to the experience of evil in the way
that symbol does to the experience of good.

This use of symbol is similar to that of Susanne Langer, a
philosopher of symbolic form who stands in the tradition
of Ernst Cassirer, a great German scholar of the early
twentieth century. Cassirer wrote the *Philosophy of Symbolic Forms* (1953-57). It was he who demonstrated
beyond question that to be human is to engage in the
process of symbolization. My immediate dependence for

65

the use of the term "symbol" is the late German-American theologian Paul Tillich, who taught during and after World War II at Union Seminary in New York, and then at Harvard Divinity School and the Divinity School of the University of Chicago.

I am also dependent upon Tillich for the particular use of the word "sign." I assume he developed this from the earlier works of Langer. In her later books Dr. Langer changes the use of sign to "signal," and "sign" becomes the equivalent of my "representation." This use of the word representation, incidentally, is rooted in the work of the father of German Idealism, Friedrich Hegel (1770-1831), who speaks of all knowledge as embodied in *Vorstellungen* ("representations"). Cassirer is dependent on Hegel, even though he is not technically a "Hegelian."

Raymond Firth, a prominent English anthropologist, discusses the nature of representations in as thorough a fashion as anyone I know. This is to be found in his book, *Symbols: Private and Public.* He adopts Langer's later use of the word "sign" for a general representation, and then divides all such signs into four categories. The first is an *index*, which indicates a sign that follows from its referent as a part from a whole, as a particular from a general, or as a precedent from an antecedent. Examples would include a signature at the end of a letter, a subject heading in a library card catalogue, or the display of an outline of a carrot and a radish to indicate the produce department of a grocery store. The second is a *signal*, which calls for a following action. Examples would include a red light that requires a car to stop, a whistle that indicates the game is to end, or a lady entering a room and bringing all the men to their feet. The third is an *icon*, which represents a sensory likeness. Vivaldi's *Four Seasons* (a musical composition), Picasso's "Guernica" (a painting of the Spanish Civil War), and Andrej Rubljow's "The Three Angelic Visitors" (a

Russian Orthodox religious painting of the Holy Trinity dating from the fifteenth century) are examples.

Firth's fourth category of signs—or as I have used the term, representations—is *symbol*. In some ways his understanding is very much like mine, except that Firth and others of his school of thought are hesitant to attribute any referent to a symbol that lies beyond our society, culture, or self. God and his works are an hypothesis that is not included in the kind of anthropology Firth does, any more than it is in much sociology and psychology today. Therefore, a symbol is seen as something created by the society or the individual, although not in an arbitrary or self-conscious manner. This is to say that no society or individual can "make" a symbol by saying, "Let's go out and whip up a few symbols today." Firth does suggest that symbols come to be constituted in the normal life of a society or individual, and therefore he would not insist as I do that they are discovered rather than invented and that they point to a referent that is ultimately transcultural and transpersonal.

One more clarification in terminology might prove helpful. I use the word "image" to indicate a potential symbol or, to return to my own use of the word, sign. Representations are *relational*. They come into being as they are employed to make sense of the experience of the subject or self. A symbol is perceived as such only as the power of the mystery of life and of God is understood within our experience. Prior to that there are many images which do not make up our meaning, but which do exist within our environment. Sometimes when an experience seems incomprehensible, what we do is go about looking for images that can become symbols and signs for that experience. In so doing we may discard many before finding just the right one, and that one becomes a representation. This is something like shopping for a new dress or suit, where we look at many possibilities (images), but choose only one or two (representations).

The purpose of this Appendix has been to help the reader who would like to inquire a bit further into my use of terms, as well as to give some basis for comparison by one who has read elsewhere in this field. The subject is a large one, it lacks systematization, but I hope that this brief analysis is helpful.

Part III

THE EXTERNAL
CONTEXT
OF MEANING

chapter SIX

Building meaning
in community

The Bible knows nothing of the individual alone with God. Quite contrary to the American notion that no one is to stand between me and my God, the Holy Scriptures testify to the fact that a countless number of persons, past and present, share with other persons their relationship to the sacred and support each of us in discovering what our experience of God means. The Letter to the Hebrews speaks of these persons as "witnesses to faith around us like a cloud" (12:1). Sociologist Robert Bellah wrote "Religious experience of all kinds is almost impossible without some form of group support." This statement is completely in accord with out best Christian insights. The task of this chapter is to point out why this is so and what it implies for our experience of God and its meaning.

What we have done in previous chapters has been to distinguish the experience of God from its meaning and analyze the internal structure of that meaning. The task before us now is to take a look at the *context* in which we construct this religious meaning. This is very similar to studying for a period the structure of the internal organs of the human body and then proceeding to analyze the ecological situation in which that body lives: such as air, climate, terrain, and population density. We are going to look, however, at only two aspects in the ecology of religious meaning: community and history.

We cannot separate the religious meaning of a person from the community of which he is a part. The community is an integral part of that individual, determining without question the form and process of his religious meaning. The community, truthfully, makes possible the experience of God itself. How it does this will be described throughout the chapter. But for the moment let me say that community makes the experience of God possible in much the same way that Nashville or its equivalent makes country music possible. This conviction concerning the function of community is especially clear in Paul, whose faith was repudiated by his own people, the Jews. He could not help but believe, in spite of this, that God had not rejected them to whom Paul owed so much in his own Christian insight (Romans 11:1-6).

It is from Paul, of course, that we get the notion of the Church as the mystical Body of Christ. He clearly based this upon the fundamental Jewish belief that a person is his community, and that a community is represented in each one of its members singly. One very familiar illustration of this deep-seated conviction in the Hebrew mind should make the point. We all recall how the young David volunteered to represent the Israelites in doing battle with the representative of the Philistines, the giant Goliath (I Samuel 17:1-54). David killed Goliath, and so the Scripture reads: "The Philistines, when they saw that their hero was dead, turned and ran." We know the story well; in fact, so well, that it probably never occurs to us to ask, "Why?" Why would two armies choose to have the fate of a battle hang on the combat between two representatives? The answer is, of course, that a man is his community and the community itself is also so much embodied in any one of its members that without question one person can conquer or die for the rest. (See Jn. 11:50, which is intended as an iron-ical prediction, and I Cor. 15:20-22.)

When Paul writes, therefore, that we all constitute the Body of Christ and that Christ represents the community of the Church, he is developing an understanding of how Christ may die and be raised for all men and how we may all partake in Christ. He is building the concept upon the fundamental insight that no one lives alone. Every individual is what he is in terms of and by virtue of the community into which he is born and reared. For the disci-ple of Christ, community is the Christian community, the Church.

The above refers specifically to the concrete theological concepts that man as community carries for the teaching of Christ's death and resurrection. My purpose in this chapter is something more general; it is to point out how commu-nity is an essential part of the construction of any religious meaning.

The Function of Community

Joachim Wach, another distinguished scholar of religious phenomena, points out that not only does all religion pos-sess cult or ritual and creed or myth, but these two always find expression in community. The three "c's" of religion—creed, cult, and community—are valid even for the person who chooses to live his life in a cave, in the middle of a desert, or on top of a pillar (after the manner of Simon Stylites and his companions in the fifth century). It is im-portant to see how this is true.

First, as I have said repeatedly, we cannot help but strive to make sense of our experience. Where, however, do we get the material from which to construct that meaning? The answer is, of course, from our community. Language, the words we use and their arrangement into sentences and paragraphs, is something given to us in our community. Patterns of behavior, art forms such as architecture and drama, and family institutions are also products of our society. If Simon Stylites could meditate for years on top of a pillar, it was because of the kind of society in which he lived. Not only did they not arrest him as dangerously demented, but they even fed him at some considerable inconvenience so that he could survive atop his perch. Simon was a product of his culture just as surely as the president of the local bank or the coach of the community's high-school football team.

The reader must understand that the very idea of "reality" is a social construction. To speak of something as *real* means that we have to be able to *speak* of it. We must have some socially agreed upon representation that *stands for* an experience and embodies it for those who have agreed upon that representation as reality. In a society that believes witches are real, there are certain experiences that the community represents by the identifiable image of a witch. There are a few people in contemporary American society who believe the earth is being visited by extraterrestrial creatures. Their problem is that the majority of people have no community image to relate to in their experience as representative of a UFO or visit from outer space. They cannot believe in this as a *reality* anymore than they can believe in witches. Community creates for us plausibility! It makes possible certain kinds of reality and renders others absurd.

Second, community is a source of authority. Let us take it out of the realm of religion for a moment and speak of the community of research chemists. It is utterly impossible for every new chemist to repeat every experiment that has produced the body of chemical knowledge. A novice chemist can hope to advance chemical knowledge only by *believing* the authority of the chemical community that has gone before. He may test certain claims, and he may eventually discover that some do not fit his data and that he will have to revise some previously accepted propositions. But as long as he is a chemist, he pursues his own interests *believing* the authority of the vast majority of chemical knowledge.

The same is true of religious knowledge. As in scientific schools of thought, there are points where the religious meaning of man suddenly takes a new direction, which we might call a "revolution" in our thinking. But even those follow upon what has gone before, with a strong dependence upon the authority of the insight of people before. No one wants to start from point zero, although some may delude themselves into thinking that is what has happened. Martin Luther, the great sixteenth-century German reformer, for example, did not break from the Roman Catholic community of which he was a part nearly so neatly as some have thought. Until the day he died, he was very much a product of the late Medieval Roman Catholicism out of which he came. In truth, the events of the fifteenth and early sixteenth centuries made possible, as well as probable, his "revolution."

Third, community is generative of new insights. Intuition requires social stimulation.* Contemporary industry relies very heavily upon what are called "think tanks." These are institutions in which communities of scholars work together, literally bouncing ideas off one another and stimulating new combinations of possible understanding. We speak of brainstorming an idea, and this is where the practice originated. It is built upon the discovery that the knowledge produced by a group is generally far greater than the sum of the knowledge brought to the group by its individual members.

* If the reader has forgotten what intuitive meaning is, he should refer back to the second chapter.

I doubt very much that the disciples of Jesus would ever have discerned the meaning of his ministry, if each one went off and thought about it by himself. It is clear that they talked among themselves, and Jesus himself is quoted as having said that wherever two or three are gathered together, there he would be—not where one person is off alone thinking solemn thoughts. Every religious movement is generated by a *group* of enthusiastic persons. This is true today, if you think of it, among members of the Jesus and neo-Pentecostal movements. The whole body of literature, for example, that those groups have developed is a result of meeting together, praying together, talking together, and writing together. It could never have been done by anyone alone.

Not only is community necessary, but there is no such thing as religious meaning without it. To pretend anything else is inevitably to live in a fantasy world, with all the dangers of exaggerated belief and action that follow from such an illusion. It must be acknowledged at the same time, however, that our community *limits* us. We see reality in a certain way because from birth our social world shaped us to see it that way, and we can move out of the norms only a little. One way of understanding maturity is to accept this and not go off on some adolescent pout over it and, at the same time, to strive to broaden our horizons and those of the community of which we are a part.

The Importance of Community

This subject is so important that I want to take a look at it from another angle that might help the reader understand why any failure to live responsibly in a community of collaborative meaning is self-destructive. Community engages us, of course, at several levels, all of which are significant to our religious meaning. The first level is that of our intimates, people with whom we associate on a personal basis from day to day. The second level is of our contemporaries known to us largely through the communication media: television, newspapers, books, magazines, radio. The third level is of our predecessors, of whom we learn by tradition. All levels play a part in the balanced construction of religious meaning for any of us.

I can best illustrate the importance of this by describing what happens when they fail to be a part of our meaning. I was attending a clergy conference in a region where for years the priests had been isolated from one another both by the accident of geography and by the failure of their leadership to develop communication. There had been no history of continuing education, and a previous bishop of the diocese, charged with bearing the apostolic tradition for his people, had apparently sought to maintain a policy of "no exchange" with his clergy. For several days I listened to these people talk, and it seemed to me their lack of a collaborative community (a natural group of people with whom we share the process of constructing meaning in a spirit of honest communication) in developing their religious meaning was seen in the following forms of destructive behavior.

First, individuals were *defensive* and repeatedly confused their emotional needs and their felt meaning with the Gospel. They claimed that their exaggerated positions were "reasonable" in the face of simple reason. For example, one person, in asserting his unwillingness to participate in a diocesan program of trial use of liturgical forms, declared his loyalty to the letter of the Book of Common Prayer. Everyone in the room knew that for at least several generations his family had used uncanonical (illegal, according to Church law) books of worship, but they were too polite to say so.

Second, there was a complete breakdown in charity as

individuals imposed upon one another stereotyped descriptions of positions to which they were hostile. To label someone is a cowardly act and makes open dialogue impossible, because the person so labeled has to spend his energies ridding himself of the stereotype rather than meeting the issue in question. For example, one priest rose and with one general "sweep" accused his opponents of being "liberals." This particular label is subject to dozens of interpretations and sheds no light on the position of other people.

Third, it was obvious that many persons present felt they had no choice but to "hang on for dear life" to a stagnant, lifeless existence where they were in the Church. The process of imagination and creation was thwarted because there was no support system to aid them in the risk that such a process necessarily requires. Consequently, they were bitter, pessimistic, and hopeless men. The Church there was a "holding operation." For example, one priest said that any change would threaten the attendence and income in his parish. The obvious conclusion is that change was forbidden and he was simply going to "endure," despite his "tipping of the hat" to the principle of change.

Fourth, the religious meaning of too many of these clergy was an anachronism. The effect was that their theology was a caricature of the past, rather than a present analysis of God's continual work among us, using the past as a resource. I was told by one cleric, for example, that he was "an unreconstructed, nineteenth-century Anglo-Catholic." It takes no genius to see the absurdity of this. Nineteenth-century persons died in the nineteenth century (or close to it) and, as late-twentieth-century men, we can only imitate them. Imitation requires understanding, which is shaped inevitably by our community of intimates and contemporaries that live today in the 1970s.

My conclusion, after this meeting, was that if we attempt

to live apart from the community in the pursuit of religious meaning, we end up defensive, living an existence, devoid of love, and adhering to a caricature of the past. This is destructive. It is destructive of the openness, the ongoing process of knowing, the deep concern for one another, and the freedom that enables us to look with hope to the future that characterizes our Lord and the Christian Gospel. The community, at all its levels, is obviously an essential part of living a Christian meaning of the experience of God, and to ignore it is to betray that which we profess to serve!

Summary

In conclusion it needs to be said that the more responsive a person is to all levels of the community, of which he is a member by virtue of his human existence, the more likely he is not to fall victim to exaggerated positions. The traditional name in the Church for such exaggerated positions is heresy, which means to choose, to choose one part of the truth and cherish it apart from the rest of the truth. It is openness to the larger community that prevents our deluding ourselves into such thinking that lacks a balanced perception and judgment.

The larger and wider our community involvement is, therefore, the better. The best known heretics through history have been men of community, but their communities have been special, little groups that have isolated themselves from the rest of mankind. Heresy has been traditionally countered in the Church by drawing together representatives from all dimensions of its life and discussing the meaning in question. One of the reasons why certain conservative Christian groups today ought to be called in question is that they avoid this kind of open contact with other Christians and, by demanding conformity to their life-style and ways of thinking, they exclude their brothers and sisters in Christ without being willing to listen to them. This may have the value of reassuring such persons that they are "something special," but it also makes it impossible for an extensive community of collaboration to function within the Church.

One of the most notable events in Christian history since the Reformation was the calling of the Second Vatican Council in 1960 by Pope John XXIII. One of the reasons why it was so important was that it opened the Roman Catholic Church to a common community of dialogue with other Christians, and we already see the fruits of that in deeper understanding among all participants of the experience of God. A more balanced and less heretical meaning is the result. John Dunne, a Roman Catholic theologian, has recently argued that the same thing can happen when we enter into conversation with other religious communities that are not even Christian in name—for example, Muslims, Buddhists, Hindus. His point is well made, if for no other reason than that it is based on the thesis of this chapter that true meaning of the experience of God is the product of clear thinking in an open community.

REVIEW QUESTIONS

1. *What does it mean to say that reality is a product of the community in which one lives?*
2. *What is belief, as distinguished from faith, and why is it important that we have a source of belief?*
3. *What happens to us when we fail to work successfully within a community of collaboration?*

chapter SEVEN

History as change

Vincent of Lerins, a fifth-century theologian, once defined the catholic or true teaching of the Church as that meaning which has been believed everywhere, always, and by all. This formula was a favorite of my own when I was growing up in the Church, for it gave me considerable comfort to feel that I knew something for certain. The only problem is that no such meaning exists. What Vincent said implies that some Christian meaning at least is implicitly in the mind of the *whole* Church *everywhere* from the beginning—and there is no evidence that this is true. Experience of God, as we saw in the first chapter, is universally the same, but the meaning with which we grasp the experience inevitably changes.

To say this, that the meaning inevitably changes, is to say that religious meaning is historical. Meaning depends on our historical situation, and history flows. It is a process. To say something is historical is to say it changes. I realize that I am repeating myself, but it is essential that the reader understand the intimate relationship between the words change, process, and history.

An ancient Greek philosopher, Heraclitus (c. 535 B.C.-475 B.C.), once wrote that no man can place his foot in the same river twice. This, in essence, is what this chapter is about. Today is not the same as yesterday, and tomorrow will be different from today. No man can stop the flow of history. Religious meaning, as we have seen, draws upon the symbols, signs, and myths of the present, or of the past as conditioned by the present, to make sense of the experience of God. The "present" from which it gathers its building materials always changes.

Vincent of Lerins was not as aware of history as we are. His inclination would be to think that what he believed as a fifth-century man was what, for example, the Fourth Evangelist believed as a first-century man. Vincent believed that Jesus was both God and man, two natures in one person. Four hundred years earlier no one believed this, not even the authors of the Gospel. How could they? They had no access to the vocabulary of fourth- and fifth-century philosophy, which, as we shall see shortly, developed the definition of a hypostasis or the kind of person who could have two natures.

Another example of how meaning changes might be helpful, for this is an extremely important point. Later than Vincent, in 1214, the Church decreed that the presence of Christ in the bread and wine consecrated in the Eucharist or Lord's Supper came about through the change in the "substance" of the bread and wine, but that their "accidents" remained the same. The terminology comes from a Greek philosopher, Aristotle, who lived in the fourth century before Christ. His writings were lost to the Western world until the 12th century when they were translated from the Arabic versions, by means of which they were transmitted through the ages. "Substance" is the name for what something "really is," and "accidents" are those characteristics that are grasped by the senses: such as color, shape, smell. For example the "substance" of a table is an internal something we might call "table-ness" whereas its "accidents" include the four legs, the walnut finish, the flat top, the smell of furniture polish.

The teaching concerning Christ's presence in the Eucharist defined in 1214 on the basis of Aristotle's terminology is called "transubstantiation," meaning literally change-of-substance (bread-ness and wine-ness). Prior to 1214 a very superstitious Church thought that if Christ were truly present in the elements of bread and wine, it meant that if one cut the bread it would bleed as physical flesh and that the wine in the chalice would taste as man's blood. The doctrine of transubstantiation was an innovation after twelve hundred years and many now consider it an absurd superstition. It was an effort, however, to use the newly discovered categories of Aristotle to overcome a crude external meaning of Christ's presence in the Eucharist. It was an important changed meaning of the external experience of God in the sacred meal.

In the sixteenth-century Reformation, men like Luther and Calvin, aware of this historical development of religious meaning, tried to overcome what they saw as a dangerous departure from the original truth that was in Jesus. They considered the teaching of the Church in the sixteenth century not only new, but unchristian. To overcome historical change they looked for an absolute in the clear and certain meaning of the Bible. The problem is that this is like trying to stand on one's own shoulders. It cannot be done. The Bible itself is a historical document. Its meaning of God changes over a period of time.

Let us look at an illustration of this point. In the Fourth Gospel we are told that the God of Jesus sent his Son not to condemn mankind but to save it (Jn. 3:17). Despite all efforts to the contrary, that meaning does not fit the God of war in the Book of Joshua, who required that all the inhabitants of Jericho except Rehab be killed, demanded the death of twelve thousand men and women of Ai, and stopped the sun in order that Joshua might slaughter more Amorites (Joshua 6:1-10:15). We find here two periods, separated by a thousand years of history, and it is no surprise that there is a considerable difference in the meaning of the experience of God between the two. This is not to imply that there is nothing of value in the Book of Joshua; it is to illustrate that change is history and the Bible is historical.

Perhaps the reader will acknowledge that this is true between the Old and the New Testament, but will argue that in the latter we get a consistent meaning that is authoritative. This is still not always the case, however, for different cultural histories among the authors of the New Testament produce an obvious difference in meaning. For example, look very briefly at the different interpretations of the disciples' post-crucifixion experience of Christ. Luke, the author of the Third Gospel and Acts, described the resurrection and, forty days later, the ascension, in order to interpret Christ's victory over death. John, the author of the Fourth Gospel, drew on some different images, creating a different meaning. By a clever use of words—one Greek word used for "crucifixion" in that Gospel also means "exaltation" (*hupsoō*) (Jn. 3:14; 8:28; 12:32, 34)—he conveys to us an understanding of the crucifixion-resurrection as a *single* event permeated with the spirit of exaltation. There is no need for an ascension symbol. The author of the Letter to the Hebrews, however, never mentions the resurrection and bases the main theme of his message on a philosophical interpretation, in accordance with the latest schools of thought, of the crucifixion and ascension (Heb. 8:1-9:28 particularly). Here are three reasonably different meanings of the one post-crucifixion experience of Christ, which are clearly indicative of the historical or changing nature of the New Testament itself.

If I argue that the Bible is historical and that meaning within it changes, the reader must not conclude that he is to reject the authority of the Holy Scriptures. I will discuss the role of the Bible as normative in the ninth chapter. The point here is to show that all meaning is historical (subject to change), and that the man of faith must learn to live within that reality when he seeks to understand the meaning of the experience of God. Put bluntly, Vincent of Lerins was dead wrong.

The Development of Meaning

In the 1973 General Convention of the Episcopal Church one of the arguments presented to the House of Deputies against allowing women to be ordained priests was that this would be the same as a recognition that doctrine develops. The speaker believed that doctrinal change is not possible in the belief of the Episcopal Church, and that to ordain women to the priesthood, for example, would surrender a fundamental article of the Church's theological position to those who teach the development of doctrine—Roman Catholics, for example. What I am saying in this chapter is that doctrine or religious meaning, to use our term for the same thing, necessarily changes or develops. Meaning is historical. As long as we keep clear the distinction between the experience of God and the meaning of that experience, this should not bother us. It certainly does not threaten the existence of the Episcopal Church or any other Church.

A good way of making this change or development clear is to go right to the heart of the matter and show how the Christian doctrine or meaning of the Trinity (the meaning of the nature of God himself) has changed or developed. The classical Christian doctrine of the Trinity is that God is *three persons in one nature*. The formula was written in the fourth and fifth centuries, when people in the Church spoke Greek or Latin; so it is important to note the Greek and Latin terms. In Greek "person" is rendered either *prosopon* or *hypostasis* and nature as *ousia*. In Latin "person" is *persona* and nature *substantia*.

The New Testament does not have a doctrine or thinking meaning of the Holy Trinity. The principal figures in those books were Jews, who believed above all in the *oneness* of God. The names themselves for the three persons of God do appear: Father, Son, and Holy Spirit. We must not, however, read a later meaning into them. It is not always clear in the New Testament whether Jesus is considered God in the same way as the Father. There are some passages that can be interpreted to mean that he is, and others that he is not, or that if he is, he is a second-class kind of God. The same opinion, condemned as a heresy almost three hundred years later, said that the Father *created* the Son before all time.

In the doctrine of the Trinity, the Holy Spirit is a person of God, just like Jesus. In the New Testament he is sometimes confused with Jesus (I Cor. 15:45; II Cor. 3:17; Gal. 4:6), sometimes the word "spirit" refers to lesser manifestations of the Father (Rev. 3:1), and sometimes the spirit appears to be an active and independent personality (Heb. 9:14). Throughout the New Testament the Holy Spirit possesses personality on some occasions, and on others it is an impersonal power operating in the lives of people, much like a fluid. It might be helpful to note that we use the word "spirit" in the latter manner also when we speak of the "spirit of patriotism."

The point is that the *experience* of God which the New Testament Church found in Jesus and the events following his Ascension (in the coming of the Holy Spirit at Pentecost in Acts 2:1-13) reveals more than can be accounted for in the Old Testament, where God is believed to be remote and totally "other" so as to protect the meaning of his oneness. For several centuries the Christian Church struggled to express the meaning of its experience in a way that would preserve this unity of God and still allow for his manifold and varied expression in our experience. After four hundred years it did this by speaking of the nature or essence (*ousia*, which means literally "being," or *substantia*, from which we get our word "substance") as one. It went on to say that this nature shows itself in three persons, which was the major change from the Old Testament.

This was also a changed meaning of God from the New Testament, which depended on the Old Testament. The controversial part of the definition was the three persons, for this ran the risk of falling into a belief in three gods. The fifth-century Church attempted to escape this by holding "nature" and "person" in tension.

Remember that one word they used for person was *hypostasis*. A *hypostasis* is that which expressed the concrete reality of something. Counterfeit money in the ancient world, for example, was said to have a *hypostasis* of base metal underneath the gold wash. In the third century the term was the same as *ousia*, meaning what something really is. However, since the word *ousia* was something defined as a result of analytical thought, as in philosophy, and *hypostasis* was more the objectivity or solidity of the fact of something's existence, by the fifth century the two words developed different meanings. An example of "a result of analytical thought" would be Aristotle's distinction between substance and accidents. "The objectivity or solidity of a fact" is illustrated by selling a "diamond ring" you inherited only to be told it is glass.

As to the other word, *prosopon*, which I indicated played a part in describing the experience of the manifestation of God's presence, its reference was the face or appearance of something. It is the "real thing," as in *hypostasis*. At least in Greek it is, for the word is to be distinguished from that for a mask (*prosopeia*). In the Latin translation this distinction slips. For in Latin it was translated by a word that originally meant mask (*persona*). Today in the psychology of the Swiss analyst Carl Jung, "persona" means the "front" or "mask" we use in meeting people. This raises the question of how "real" the three persons were in the fifth-century *Latin* Church.

The point of all this word study is to show that the fifth-century Church, in defining the experience of God as of one possessing a single *ousia* or nature in three *hypostases* or *prosopa* or persons, it was trying its best to preserve the unity of God while doing justice to three distinct, personal manifestations of that God in the Father, the Son, and the Holy Spirit. This was a clear development or change from the meaning of the New Testament Church. It did not stop changing here, however. This is seen in what happened through subsequent history to the word "person." The word began to change in what it represented almost as quickly as it was defined. It moved away from an almost masklike concrete reality, which possessed the thinnest possible distinction from the other two persons of the Godhead, and became more and more a word representing a clear, separate self-consciousness, standing all alone. As a result, the underlying essence of the oneness of God was progressively obscured. By the time we come to the present a "person" has become a discrete individual, independent of others in terms of its emotional history, intellectual conviction, and active will. The "nature" of a person is his self-consciousness, which he alone possesses. The notion of the oneness of God lying in a transpersonal (above personal distinctions) nature becomes an abstraction for which we find nothing in the meaning of our experience.

Let us summarize a couple of general principles seen in this extended example of the change or development in the Christian doctrine of God as Trinity. What, in effect, happens in the development of meaning is twofold, with an additional very important side effect or by-product. First, as we reflect on our experience through the centuries, we are more and more able to clarify and share its meaning. The explicit fifth-century meaning of the Trinity is implicit in the New Testament Church, but it is obscure and not adequately shared in the early documents. Second, the referent of the words we use to clarify and share our experience slips out from under these very words in time. The word "person" refers to something different in man's experience in the fifth century from what it does in the twentieth century.

At this moment, it is most important for us to identify the side effect to which I refer. Our emotional investment or felt meaning comes to be placed, not in the experience but in the words that make up the internal structure of the meaning of the experience. We will fight "to the death" over the words, sometimes with little reference to the experience itself. For example, at the 1973 General Convention of the Episcopal Church I heard someone state with some emotion his unhappiness at the change, in a new translation of the Nicene Creed, of the word "substance" into "being." ("We believe in one Lord, Jesus Christ, . . . one in Being with the Father" as compared to "And in one Lord Jesus Christ, . . . Being of one substance with the Father.") The reply to this person was that our English word "substance" is a translation of the Latin *substantia*, which was, in turn, a rather poor translation of the Greek original *ousia* ("being"). The new translation, while not perfect, is far better than the old one. Aside from making ourselves ridiculous, this investment in words rather than experience is self-defeating and destructive of God's purpose.

The Life-span of Symbols and Signs

In this context, when we speak of the historical nature of meaning we are referring to the internal structure of meaning, namely, the symbols and signs, the rituals, the propositions, the systems, and the myths that go together to form the meaning of God. It needs to be clearly understood that the various kinds of material from which we construct such meaning do *not* have identical life-spans. On the one hand, the doctrine of the Trinity, which I have discussed at length in the previous section, has a relatively long life-span compared, for example, to the sixteenth-century teaching of John Calvin—that man is predestined by God to heaven or to hell. Calvin's teaching is believed by far fewer people today than, say, a hundred years ago, and actually had an active life of only about three hundred years. On the other hand, however, the belief in the divine intervention in history by a "heavenly man" of some kind—in terms of which we Christians understand Jesus—goes back into the dim prehistory of man and is a much older meaning than the belief that God is three *prosopa* or persons in one *ousia*, nature or being.

It possibly follows that symbols have a longer life-span than signs, and that myths tend to retain their original significance for us longer than theological systems built upon the conceptual use of propositions. For example, a basic symbol to which we have referred before in man's life is the sacred meal. Its power survives from the earliest history of man until now. The doctrine of the transubstantiation, which involves two signs (substance and accidents), had an effective life from the twelfth to the eighteenth centuries. The idea of substance is generally, though not exclusively, rejected by philosophy since then. Then again, the myth of the death and resurrection of the "heavenly man," which is thousands of years old and which takes on historical reality in Jesus, lives on today, while a theological system such as the *Systematic Theology* of Paul Tillich, who died within the last decade, is already open to question, in spite of his greatness.

Of course, symbols themselves have varying life-spans.

The old wagon pulled by a mule, which in 1968 carried the body of the American Christian martyr, Martin Luther King, to his grave, is a symbol. Its life-span, however, is no more than two hundred years, much shorter than the sacred meal to which we referred. The American myth of the technological man, who conquers the world and achieves salvation or wholeness by his control of creation through manipulation and production for his own ends, is a modern story, much briefer in history than the myth of the "heavenly man" who dies and is resurrected for the salvation of man.

Symbols and signs, myths and systems have a relationship to culture. Some live above culture and survive from period to period with little apparent change. When there are times, like our own, when culture is broken and fragmented, there are no universal *cultural* signs and systems on which to draw in order to effect a *common* meaning. Then it becomes particularly important to identify those transcultural symbols and myths on which we can root the meaning of our experience of God. It is, in my mind, most important, therefore, that we today discern the fundamental symbol power in our rites, such as the Eucharist and Baptism. It is necessary for this reason, I believe, that we take the function of myth seriously and identify those that are operative in our life.

Summary

We come now to the end of our concern with the environment or context out of which we construct the meaning of the experience of God. In the next three chapters I will discuss the role, in speaking of God, of certain specific elements in the Christian tradition. Here Jesus, the Bible, and classical theology will be considered in the light of all we have discussed to this point. This is the next obvious step, as we have moved from the absolute of the experience of God to the internal structure of religious meaning, and on to the context of constructing that meaning.

Before moving on, however, one clear implication of this chapter needs to be emphasized. If Heraclitus was right, as I believe he was and as I have illustrated throughout this chapter—namely, no man can put his foot in the same river twice—then it is a futile effort to attempt to find some Golden Age of the past and try to live in it. This is what the German martyr from World War II, Dietrich Bonhoeffer, called "the leap of death." We are "dead" when we abandon the now to live in the ashes and dead bones of the past. We have no choice but to live in the present. Nostalgia is, at best, only a harmless diversion, and at worst, a totally destructive abdication of our God-given responsibility.

For example, being "like Jesus" does not mean living like a first-century, Galilean peasant. That is impossible by definition of time and, for most of us, of space. I have a friend who speaks of "bathrobe Christianity." He has in mind those Sunday School Christmas pageants where the boys are dressed in their fathers' bathrobes in order to look like the first-century shepherds. In fact, we know that first-century shepherds did not appear this way and all we are doing is playing "let's pretend." Any effort to live in the past is a game of "let's pretend," and its meaning cannot be taken seriously for today. Whether it be the first, fourth, thirteenth, or sixteenth century—or whatever period somebody may choose—we cannot go back. We cannot return to the Garden of Eden to escape the agony and toil of this present age. We can only live out of the past in the present for the sake of the future.

REVIEW QUESTIONS

1. *What are the implications for religious meaning in saying that no man can set his foot in the same river twice? Why does this make Vincent of Lerins wrong?*
2. *How is the doctrine of the Trinity an illustration of one stage in the development of a meaning of God?*
3. *What does it mean to say that symbols and myths generally have a longer life-span than signs and systems of theology?*

Part IV

THE SUBSTANCE OF CHRISTIAN MEANING

chapter EIGHT

Jesus

Nothing that I have said in the previous seven chapters can be considered specifically Christian. The nature of the experience of God, the internal structure of the meaning of God, and the context for the construction of that meaning all apply to the fulfillment of man's religious nature in terms of any belief system—Hindu, Buddhist, Muslim, naturalist. I now want to move from this general consideration to discuss specific Christian meaning in terms of what we have already analyzed. Certainly I have written the previous chapters as a Christian, and obviously I have used illustrations from my own belief. My purpose from here on, however, is to help us take seriously the content of Christian belief; and, to see it, as a result of what I have already written, as the response of a given community in history, who in all faith are convinced that their experience is the fulfillment of all mankind's longing to make sense of his life.

The content of our Christian meaning may be explored in many ways. Here we shall briefly touch upon three key areas: Jesus, the Bible, and doctrine or theology as dogma and system. Obviously, nothing that is done here purports to be exhaustive. Having read the previous seven chapters, the reader will find a way of approaching these critical areas of our belief in a manner that enables him to find, in their light, power and reason in his life and a continued hope in God's purpose for us all.

The New Testament says of Jesus that he is "the same yesterday, today, and forever" (Heb. 13:8). It also says in Luke's Gospel that Jesus *grew* in the knowledge and favor of God (Lk. 2:52). Jesus has always been the "same" and he "grows." Is this not a contradiction? How can he both remain who he is and yet develop? It is in this apparent contradiction, however, that we have an essential, fundamental claim of the Christian experience and meaning.

In this chapter I intend to speak of Jesus as symbol, sign, and myth. *I am not so much concerned with a theological definition of what was or is the nature of Jesus, but with his meaning or function for us!* In other words, as throughout this book, I am starting from below, not from above. That is, I do not claim to have a "pipe line" to God's mind and understanding of Jesus, but I am seeking to understand him as he has appeared among men. All religions have symbols, signs, and myths, which make up their meaning of God. Christianity, however, claims that these three categories which speak of the infinite and eternal reality of God find in Jesus embodiment or "flesh" (the word "incarnation," in terms of which we speak of God coming to us in Jesus, means in-*flesh*-ment). In the midst of history, which we have already seen as change by definition (see Chapter Seven), the unchanging purpose of God becomes evident. Jesus Christ, the New Testament says, is the same always, but it also says that the historical person, Jesus, the Galilean peasant, changes. That is the strange contradiction to which the Christian community witnesses.

There has always been a tendency to try to get off the horns of that dilemma. There have been many who have said that Jesus was just a good man, like many other good men (Moses, Mohammed, Zoroaster, Francis of Assisi). If we claim only this, however, there is in him no real presence with power of God's purpose for us. Others have suggested that Jesus need never have actually lived, historically speaking, because we need only the idea of his perfect life to call us to wholeness. This also leads to despair, because ideas are mental abstractions and our life is much more than a notion in our mind. Our life is one of concrete things: blood and bone, dirt and heat, excruciating pain, and exhilarating pleasure. If we are to be made whole it must be in terms of what we know to be our entire life: body, emotions, mind, and spirit lived in a changing world of nature and society.

We insist as Christians that the whole of life is real and God's creation. Therefore, we not only stand in opposition to religions like Buddhism and Hinduism, we are faced with the problem of how Jesus can be both the same and grow. It is the issue of God and history. Part of the answer will be developed in the rest of this chapter, but now this one point might be made. The life of Jesus—the whole thing— is a gift of God to man in terms that man can understand; namely, his finite, everyday existence. It is a gift that proclaims with power at *one* point in history the goal of *all* history. Christianity believes the world is going somewhere. Jesus apparently spoke of this "somewhere" in very concrete terms as the Kingdom of God or heaven. That is a kind of *social* or *community* image. The Fourth Evangelist called it eternal life, which is more personal and abstract. The point is that the world and every one of us in it has a destiny—a "somewhere" to go. The gift of God's life in Jesus was to offer us the promise and means of achieving that goal. Whether we are the whole world or one individual, Jesus is the foretaste of our goal in life, where the many fragments of existence become one in God.

Jesus as Symbol

Christians believe that Jesus is the primary and supreme symbol of God. Many religions have a "primal event," and Jesus' life is that for the Christian community. (A primal event is that great occasion when whatever happened to form the community, the ritual, and the myth occurred.) Sometimes we speak of the Church as the "primary sacrament" or symbol of God in Christ, but that is only an extension of our belief that God was and is in Christ, reconciling or calling us to him (II Cor. 5:19). The Church is the "body," the historical presence of the eternal Christ, in the world, since the historical Jesus returned to the presence of God the Father.

I used the expression "eternal Christ." What does that mean? Many religions have within them the belief that there exists a prototypical or cosmic man, who is the actual, real embodiment of what you and I are to be when we are whole. There was a Buddhist tradition that man in the beginning was both male and female at the same time (this is called an "androgyne" from the two Greek words for man, [*anēr, andros*] and woman [*gynaix, gynaikos*]) and once lived in Paradise. He fell into the created world, became divided into male and female, and has suffered from passion ever since. His life of passion is a struggle to recover the original state. The story of Adam and Eve in the Book of Genesis is seen in some Near Eastern traditions as an account of such an *Urmensch*, a German word meaning the primal or prototypicial man. Our goal is to return to the Garden of Eden.

There is a widespread tradition of the "heavenly man," which may have been in the mind of the author of the Book of Daniel, when he speaks of the coming of the "son of man." This was part of the Jewish anticipation of the Messiah, a Jewish word meaning the "anointed one," and of which "Christ" is simply a Greek translation. This was the anticipation of the coming of the "heavenly man," who would somehow set things right. To speak of the "eternal Christ" is to speak of Jesus as the fulfillment of many different kinds of longing for the perfect man, a gift from God to enable us to become as such a man, living in harmony with God. The feeling of anticipation which many of us have around Christmas is a particular form of that same longing of the Jewish people fot the Messiah. As the New English Bible puts it, "The people were on the tiptoe of expectation" (Lk. 3:15), in expectation for the eternal or cosmic Christ to come among us.

Of course, this expectation of what the Christ or the heavenly man is like takes many forms. We would expect this of a symbol. (See Chapter Three.) Because the Jews at the time of Jesus' birth were experiencing the rule of the Roman Empire. They thought of the Messiah or Christ coming to do what they believed they needed most: liberation from the Romans. He should have been an earthly king who drove out the hated oppressor. If one does not understand this, he will fail to see why on the first Palm Sunday they hailed Jesus as a king and five days later insisted that he be crucified (Lk. 19:35-40, 23:13-25). There is no fury quite like that of a disappointed lover! Jesus did not *fit* the expectations of the Jews. He never "fits."

People have been interpreting Jesus in terms of their own needs for centuries. To the early Christian he was the compassionate Good Shepherd, leading them to their heavenly reward amidst persecution. The earliest representation in art we have of Jesus is on the wall of a catacomb (an underground cemetery in Rome), where he appears as a shepherd. The Byzantine or Eastern Church from 500 to 1500 depicted Jesus in mosaics (bits of colored, chipped ceramic). In the Church at Daphni, Greece, the mosaics on the walls show a fascinating transition from this gentle shepherd Jesus, in a pastoral, Hellenistic style, to, in the apex of the dome, an extremely stern notion of our Lord as the judge of the living and the dead. This latter image is called the *pantocrator*, the "ruler of all." For this artist, Jesus must have been a very stern ruler indeed. One critic describes the Daphni *pantocrator* as a "forceful depiction," "the least 'amiable' of all Byzantine images of Christ"; and another critic speaks of it as "terrible in its grim severity."

The late medieval Church of the fourteenth and fifteenth centuries endured the stark horror of the so-called "black death," a plague that was carried by the fleas on rats that had traveled on the trading ships from the Orient. One-third to one-half of the population of western Europe was wiped out by this gruesome disease. For such people Jesus was the tortured figure on the cross, the man who shared their agony and yet saved them. In the nineteenth century, when men as gentlemen repressed their strong feelings, Jesus was the pale Galilean, the epitome of the sweet, kind man, who suffered injustice as if he were above it all. Today we have the Jesus of the Broadway shows, *Jesus Christ, Superstar* and *Godspell*. Here, as a kind of cosmic "hippy," he embodies the longings of the youth culture for authenticity amid the *kitsch* of our plastic technology.

Jesus is all these things and, most important, more. He never fits our particular desires for him, and yet he makes our life have value in the midst of our particular needs. Dorothy Sayers, an English author writing mystery stories and theology (a not uncommon ambiguous combination), said that it was the *incongruity* (the not-fitting-ness) of Jesus that was and is his power. He conforms to no simple categories, but embodies a great number of different denotations and connotations. He evokes all kinds of feelings, some perhaps contradictory (as, for example, when the Jews hailed him as king and then demanded his death). This is, of course, the definition of a symbol. (See Chapter Three.)

Think of the strange fascination of the man! No one knows quite why he draws them to himself. The elders in the Temple listened to the boy in amazement (Lk. 3:47), James, John, Andrew, and Peter gave up a good fishing

business to follow him along the dusty road (Mt. 4:18-22);
Pontius Pilate's wife warned her husband to avoid this
strange man (Mt. 27:19); and the distinguished Jewish
scholar, Paul of Tarsus, threw over a "successful career" to
become a missionary and a martyr for him. Why? There is
no way of explaining this, except to say that Jesus is the
symbol of God's presence, God's solicitation of us into
being. He possesses the magnetic power of the symbol,
whose very incongruity draws us into participation with
God and yet remains a part of the mystery of God. To attempt to reduce the experience of Jesus to a simple definition is—thank God—doomed to failure. He is all things to
all men and the manifestation of the will of God. That is
his power. He is the heavenly man in the flesh of man.

Jesus as Sign

When I speak of Jesus as sign I am referring to what he
tells us, not what the Church says about him (which is related to the next two chapters). A sign, as we should recall
(see Chapter Four), has more clarity than a symbol, as it
becomes a means for sharing with one another the quest for
the truth. Signs define our action, which is to say that they
tell us what to do. A symbol is ambiguous, but Jesus as a
sign should direct our lives. The Fourth Evangelist speaks
of Jesus as the truth (Jn. 8:31-32; 14:6; 18:38). What does
that mean?

Did you ever ask yourself the question: What would
Jesus think of me doing this? Or what does Jesus want me
to do? This is an effort to answer what the truth is. Sometimes the voice of Jesus may get confused with that of the
memory of our mother or father. There are some people
who believe Jesus does not want them to drink alcoholic
beverages, despite the fact that in the New Testament the
author of a letter to Timothy tells him to take some wine

for the sake of his digestion (I Tim. 5:23). Some people think that Jesus was the first capitalist, while others invoke him as the authority for revolutionary action. Roman Catholics believe that he established the Church with the Bishop of Rome as his special representative (based on Mt. 16:18), whereas other New Testament scholars do not think that our Lord even intended to found an institutional Church (believing that the Kingdom was to come momentarily).

The problem of what Jesus-as-sign means is that our best records of him are in the New Testament and he himself wrote nothing. In fact, the New Testament was written originally in Greek, and Jesus, to the best of our knowledge, spoke only Aramaic, the language of the Jews at that time. We do not know even if Jesus knew how to write his own language. How well could Jesus' teaching be remembered? We have no assurance that we have reasonably accurate quotations from Jesus in the New Testament. The oldest book in the New Testament is probably I Thessalonians, and may have been composed about twenty years after Jesus' death and resurrection. Paul, who wrote I Thessalonians, tells us he never met Jesus in the flesh (I Cor. 9:1 refers to 15:8, the vision on the road to Damascus); and the oldest Gospel account, Mark, is fifteen to twenty years later than I Thessalonians. In fact, many of the sayings attributed to Jesus appear to be part of the common wisdom of the Jewish people, and can be found in literature that predates his life.

The problem I am pointing to is that of the historical Jesus. In the last hundred and fifty years scholars have struggled to capture what Jesus really did and said. It is so difficult to get back behind the New Testament, with all the layers of interpretation imposed by authors and editors, to the actual man, Jesus of Nazareth, that a few researchers have suggested that perhaps Jesus never lived and that he is the product of the minds of people like Paul. That is an extreme point of view, which I think would destroy the heart of the Christian witness, if it were true. I cite it to warn the reader about assuming too easily that he knows the truth in Jesus-as-sign.

I do think, however, that there are some elements of Jesus-as-sign that we can recover. They are not anything as culturally determined or trivial as whether or not we should drink, at what age we should baptize, or what is the precise nature of the Church's government. The signs in Jesus are more general and profound. I think there is little question but that Jesus taught that a new age was coming in which a new pattern of behavior was demanded. Repentence is a call to *change*, to become a different kind of man. Paul Minear, an eminent New Testament scholar, has described some of the characteristics of that new man as Jesus saw him. I find what he has to say most helpful.

The new man in Christ, as Minear sees the New Testament reflecting Jesus' intent, is one who says what he means. He is unequivocal in speech. There is a hidden quality to his relationship with God. Love is the highest value, and he will give of all he has to that end. The community comes before the individual, and he will sacrifice all for the well-being of his brother. He is one who anticipates that God will meet his every need, and therefore he is both carefree and prayerful. Finally, he shares the gifts of God, including the gift of the "heavenly man" in Jesus.

There is no question but that these propositions describe a life-style that is not limited to one culture. It is the task of the Church in every age to work out the details of such a pattern, which is what I mean when, with James Gustafson, a theologian teaching at the University of Chicago, I speak of the Christian congregation as a "community of moral discourse." The relationship is, however, one of seeing Jesus as a sign for our life and yet not claiming for our interpretation of that sign in a given age anything more than the belief that when we gather in Christ's name and are open to his truth, he will guide our specific conclusions in the light of his more universal teaching. I do not see how it could be otherwise.

Jesus as Myth

I refer now to the *events* of Jesus' life, such as his birth, his miracles, his death and resurrection, his ascension. These are stories about Jesus, little dramatic instances, which have become for many people tests of whether or not they accept the power of Jesus to make them whole on the basis of believing that they "really happened." I think this is an unfortunate, even tragic, clouding of the real issue. Remember that a myth is a true story (see Chapter Five); nevertheless some myths are no more than stories of our imagination (Adam and Eve, for example), and others actually happened in history (you could have taken movies of the drama if you had been there). The important thing is that Jesus must have a mythical form to be what the Church believes him to be: the experience of God. Myth as true story reveals to us the mystery of God in a way that shapes our life as nothing else could. That is its all-important power!

Jesus is a historical fulfillment of mankind's most powerful myths. This is part of what God's gift of his life in Jesus, as a living, concrete man, means. It happens that the whole notion of the "heavenly man" coming among us by means of God's commerce with a virgin is common in ancient literature. We know it in the story of Jesus as the Virgin Birth or, more accurately, Conception. Miracles as signs of God's powerful presence making men whole is an almost universal expectation in religious stories. There is no more profound mythic motif in countless religions around the world than the conflict-victory themes of the death and resurrection of the divine being or heavenly man. A very sophisticated myth of movement from mortality to immortality, which did not get much development in later Western Christianity, is also related to Jesus in the Epistle to the Hebrews.

The life of Jesus is surrounded by mythic interpretation, and his life itself clearly participates in universal mythic forms. I happen to believe that some of them are clearly historical. I do not, however, have to believe that *all* the myths related to Jesus are historical events, to accept the truth of all those myths, or to insist that Jesus as the presence of God among us is historical fact. Jesus was crucified, died, was buried, and was raised from the grave. This central reality of his life gives specific form to a formless intuition that religious man has had for countless centuries. Many devout Christians believe that neither the Virgin Conception nor the Ascension were historical incidents, but that both were myths that reveal to us a profound truth about the nature of Jesus' life. This is to say, in the first instance, that his life was a unique and altogether singular gift of God's presence among us; and in the second place, that Jesus lives now and calls us by the power of his life, death, and resurrection to be like him. He *is* the cosmic Christ, the heavenly man, a symbol to which the myth gives narrative form.

What I said about myth in the fifth chapter, and about the disruptive interpretations of those who do not grasp the function of myth, need to be kept in mind at this point, but I will end this chapter on a more positive note. Remember that ritual reenacts the myth and, by the use of symbol, evokes the feeling of the primal event of that community's faith. For us Christians that symbol is preeminently Jesus and the myth of his death and resurrection. Our life as Christians is found in the community, which gathers to celebrate the rite of Jesus' passage through death into the new life. This is how the Christian participates in the vital reality of his religion; there is no other way for a person who takes Jesus seriously. The tragedy of so much religious reform in the history of Christianity has been that people have denied this involvement for themselves and their followers and, as a consequence, have drifted from the mainsteam of the Christian witness. They have made the mistake of thinking of Jesus as sign, without realizing that the power of the sign is the symbol and myth.

Summary

There is a tradition in Christian thought: *lex credendi lex orandi*. That means that we believe what we pray. Another way of putting it is that sign follows symbol. Jesus is the standard or norm for the Christian of all that we as mankind believe about God. All other religious meaning, in other words, has to be measured against what the experience of Jesus means. That meaning, however, begins in Jesus as symbol and myth and then moves to sign, although propositional truth is necessary. What Jesus taught is important not for its own sake, but because of its source in the symbol of the person of God which we experience in his life. For the Christian, speaking of God begins in the experience of the symbol of Jesus. Furthermore, when we speak of having "a personal relationship with Jesus," the only place to root that relationship is in the symbolic reality of Christ, as cosmic, heavenly man. Anything else is idle "Jesusolatry," an attempt to live in the midst of this age within a remote, first-century country.

REVIEW QUESTIONS

1. *What does it mean to say that Jesus is first and foremost a symbol or sacrament of God for us? How does this relate to the many different interpretations placed upon him through the centuries?*
2. *What is the problem with understanding the sign value of Jesus? How does this relate to the chapter on history?*
3. *What does it mean to say that the life of Jesus fulfills the most profound myth of human mystery? How does this differ from saying that Jesus is the fulfillment of the Jewish Law? How does this help relate Jesus to non-Christian religions?*

chapter NINE

The Bible

Many of us remember these familiar lines from Sunday School.

> Jesus loves me, this I know
> For the Bible tells me so.

We have just been thinking about Jesus, but for many Christians the Bible lies behind what we know of Jesus and is the central source of Christian meaning. In a sense this is true, but there is more than one way of looking at it.

It was the life, death, and resurrection of our Lord that called the Church into being. That is what is meant by saying that Jesus is the "primal event" of Christianity. The Christian community that grew after the first Easter and the Pentecost experience (as recorded in Acts 2:1-41) existed because of its experience of the Christ. There is no question but that many evangelists for Jesus, such as Peter and Paul, documented the meaning of our Lord's coming from the Jewish Scriptures of that day (roughly equivalent to the Old Testament). The Bible *as we know it*, however, did not exist until centuries later.

What created the Bible? To ask that question is to inquire what makes these writings Holy Scripture, the sacred books of the Christian Church. Some people would answer that question by saying it is the Word of God. This may mean to them that God literally dictated the precise words. Such a suggestion makes for a very strange idea of God.

We know that these writings are the product of a thousand years of Jewish and Christian thought (generally from the eighth century B.C. to the second century A.D.), and are written in three different languages. We have all kinds of bits and pieces of manuscripts of the Bible with slightly varying texts, and yet we cannot claim for any version of the Bible or ancient manuscript that it is *the* original. Furthermore, most of us read the Bible in translation, and it is impossible to make an exact rendition of meaning from one language into another. This is why, for example, it is naive to think that the Authorized or King James version of the English Bible, dating from 1611, is the word-for-word inspiration of the Holy Spirit. The Bible is not the Bible because it is the result of God's dictation.

Others have suggested that the Bible is what it is because of the special class or category of the people who wrote it. In the case of the New Testament it would imply they were people who knew our Lord in the flesh. If not a "special class," they were persons who had a special, intimate relationship with God. The fact is that we do not know who wrote most of the books of the Bible. For example, David did not write most—if any—of the Psalms, as we once claimed. The Book of Esther lacks any obvious inspiration. In its Hebrew form it never mentions God. The Song of Songs is a lovely Jewish marriage song, but quite worldly. The New Testament books were written by all kinds of people, including Paul, who as I noted in an earlier chapter, never saw Jesus before his resurrection. In the case of at least two of the Gospels, we do not know their writers. One of them, the Fourth, was certainly not written much before A.D. 90, which makes it highly unlikely that the author knew Jesus of Nazareth personally. II Peter was probably not written until a hundred years after Jesus' resurrection. The Bible is not what it is because of the special category or even the holiness of the authors.

In fact, all the books in the Bible were not generally

agreed upon until the end of the fourth century A.D., more than three hundred years after Jesus. The oldest, nearly complete manuscript we have of the New Testament, which dates from the fourth century, lacks the Book of Revelation and has a writing called the Epistle of Barnabas. When consensus did come as to the twenty-seven books of the New Testament, we can only say it was because *it was the apparent consensus of the Church that it accurately represented its experience of God in Christ.*

The situation with the Old Testament is somewhat different. The early Church accepted the Jewish Scriptures, as they were found in a Greek translation, called the Septuagint (meaning "seventy," because the tradition was that seventy scholars translated them from Hebrew into Greek). This version of the Old Testament consists of the thirty-nine books of the Protestant Old Testament, plus thirteen of the fourteen books of what is called by Anglicans (Episcopalians in the United States) the *Apocrypha*. The word *apocrypha* means "hidden," on the theory that the authors are unknown—an idle point, since we know few other authors in the Bible. (II Esdras from the Apocrypha is *not* in the original Old Testament.) The Roman Catholics still use this Old Testament. Since the sixteenth century Protestants do not have as large an Old Testament on the theory that only books originally written in Hebrew should be included, as representing the experience of the Jews before Christ. The Anglicans have kept the Apocrypha, however, as a "secondary source" of the scriptural material.

My desire is to make clear to the reader why the Bible is what it is. The conclusion is that *the Bible is the Church's book*. It is the collection of writings which *the Church has agreed* embodies in propositional form a normative meaning of its experience of God in Christ. (By "normative" I mean the standard by which we judge all other meaning.)

There is no other reason in the final analysis for the selection of the content. Therefore the Church and its Lord, who called it into being, is prior to the Bible in the sense that the Bible is the product of the community's experience of Jesus.

Of course, the Bible serves to illuminate, confront, and challenge our experience today. In this sense the Holy Scriptures are prior to our contemporary life in the Church. The reading of the Bible and preaching from the Bible addresses man today, judges him, and calls him into a faith in God and his Son. When I say that I know Jesus loves me because the Bible tells me so, and if this is not intended to be all-inclusive, I am speaking the truth. (There are other sources of this knowledge, such as our fellow Christians, participation in the sacraments, and reading of religious literature.) It is essential that we do not downgrade the profound and central importance of the Bible, therefore, as it engages us in a powerful form with the authoritative meaning of the Church—in the sense that it both expresses and feeds the Christian community's experience of its Lord.

The Bible is a narrative; it is propositional meaning. I said in the fourth chapter that it is very easy to misunderstand the function of such meaning. One way of appreciating the role of the Holy Scriptures in the specifically Christian content of religious meaning is to analyze how the three functions discussed previously are found in the Bible. Let us do that now.

Scriptures as a Point of View

As I have already said, some propositions simply state how we perceive ourselves in the world. They may be statements concerning ethical matters; such as "It is not right to rob banks." Or they may express only a particular view of the world; for example, "Summer is better than winter." Independent of our subjective judgment, there is no way of proving either statement right or wrong, true or false. Yet such points of view are vitally important, because they define many times the way in which we relate to ourselves, to other people, and to the world in general.

One very clear and extremely important point of view that pervades the entire Bible is the belief that the Hebrews or Jews (the name for the same people after the fall of the Northern Kingdom in 722 B.C.), followed by the Church, are the "chosen people" of God. In Deuteronomy, a book dating from the seventh century B.C., it is written of the Israelites—another name for the Hebrews, referring to them as the sons of Israel or Jacob, who was the third of the great patriarchs and whose twelve sons fathered the twelve tribes (see Gen. 35:9-10, 23-26; 49:1-33)—"The Lord your God chose you out of all nations on earth to be his special possession" (Deut. 7:6). The Jews believed themselves to have a special compact or covenant with God, which we call the Old Testament or Covenant.

The early Christians believed this divine election was transferred to the Church, which is the whole thrust of Paul's famous argument about Abraham and the justification by faith (Romans 3:21-4:25). It is no accident that Luke sees the Church as founded in the twelve apostles, who are the successors of the twelve tribes (see Lk. 6:13; 18:31; Acts 1:23-26). The transfer of election to the Church is given a cosmic meaning when the author of the letter to the Ephesians writes of the Christian community "In Christ he chose us before the world was founded" (Eph. 1:4). (The word "cosmic" refers to all of the created universe as possessing an order which is given it by God.) This change in the covenant relationship was considered, from the viewpoint of the Christians, the *New*

Testament or Covenant, which it was believed Jeremiah promised (see Jer. 31:31-34).

The importance of this self-understanding, first for the action of the Jews and then of the Christian Church, is obvious. It kept the Jews going amid incredible hardship. The books of Ruth and Jonah, for example, are expressive of a debate that raged in the Jewish community as to whether Jews might intermarry. Because of their chosen status, if they married non-Jews they might lose their purity as a people, or even their identity. Such an attitude depended on one's "point of view." The Church has argued the meaning of election (the act of God choosing us) for centuries, and the theology of the Reformed tradition (Presbyterianism and Congregationalism) was shaped because of a particular interpretation rooted in the sixteenth-century reformer John Calvin.

Another biblical point of view, which has come under considerable question recently, is rooted in the verse: "So God created man . . . , blessed them and said to them, 'Be fruitful and increase, fill the earth and subdue it, rule over the fish of the sea, the birds of the heaven, and every living thing that moves on the earth' " (Genesis 1:27-28). The effect of this aggressive outlook, according to some contemporary theologians, has been to encourage the Christian culture to abuse the creation and to despoil our natural resources. It has failed to encourage a sense of communion between man and nature, which is typical of some other religions. It is suggested that as a result we find the West faced with a pressing ecological crisis.

The Ten Commandments and the Beatitudes are both examples of the Bible as expressive of a point of view. As Christians we may give them the authority of God, but there is no way of proving their truth. "You shall not make wrong use of the name of the Lord your God" (Deut.

5:11) is generally to prohibit certain scatological or blasphemous language. This is a point of view consistent with my own upbringing, and perhaps the reader's, but there is nowhere for us to appeal for an absolute judgment on its truth. It could be said to be no more than a question of "taste." "How blest are those of a gentle spirit" (Mt. 5:5) is an appealing sentiment in which I concur, but I have no final argument with those who disagree, except my own opinion, shaped by a Christian family in a Christian tradition. It ultimately boils down to a personal outlook.

I offer these illustrations of the Scriptures as a point of view, not to refute anything but to suggest that we understand their function. These propositions do not state something subject to verification from the data of experience; they are important interpretations in the Judaeo-Christian tradition of what life is all about, interpretations that guide our style of life. They are no more than this, but this in itself is essential to a meaningful existence.

Scripture as Statement of Fact

We find in the Bible many simple historical events or, as some say, "brute facts." They are subject to verification as much as any other chronicle of the past. There is little question that there was a Jesus of Nazareth who was crucified under a petty Roman official named Pontius Pilate. Paul went to Rome. The author of Revelation, who probably bore the common name John, may well have been imprisoned upon the barren island of Patmos, from which he wrote to the churches in seven Asia Minor cities (Rev. 1:4, 9). Turning to the Old Testament, we find no reason to question the listing of the kings of Israel: Saul, David, and Solomon; as well as the kings of the Northern and Southern Kingdoms. Some of the events related to each of them are undoubtedly verifiable. Despite some theories to the contrary, Moses is generally judged to be a real figure in history.

We could go on listing such "brute facts" found in the Scriptures, but these are only of incidental importance to other propositions in the Scriptures which, I would argue, are also statements of fact in that they may be rationally judged as true in terms of our experience. There are certain theological propositions, conceptual interpretations of God and man of a kind that will occupy our concern in the last two chapters.* For the present it is sufficient to illustrate how they are an essential part of the Bible.

Some time in the fifth century B.C., a nameless Jewish prophet, living in exile with his countrymen, wrote in poetic language of the oneness of God, who alone created the heavens and the earth and who rules all the people that live in the world. He identified this one God with the Jewish Lord, Yahweh (Isaiah 41:1-16). Despite the poetic form, this is a theological proposition, somewhat unique (although not entirely) in that day and time. It is the assertion that transcendent reality is one, is the source of all that is, and plays a guiding hand in the affairs of man. The Hebrews did not always believe this. There is evidence that in earlier times they simply thought their God was their own peculiar Lord, perhaps better than any other, and that it was all right for Gentiles to worship their own gods (who were perhaps lesser demonic beings). This seems to be the implication of the story of the healing of the Assyrian officer, Naaman, by Elisha (II Kings 5:1-19).

This theological concept of the oneness of God, who is our sustaining creator, seems to me a *reasonable judgment* from our experience. This is, it should be noted, not to say we can *prove* such a god's existence. David Miller, a theological scholar, has recently written a book in which he

---

* Remember that a "concept" is the result of thinking and is the kind of proposition that makes up such meaning.

describes himself as a "polytheist." At face value this would mean he believed in "many gods." If this is what he intends, I would be willing to argue against him. The oneness of life seems evident to me, and from that it is reasonable to argue for one source of it all.

Another example of a theological concept, this time related to the nature of man before God, is Paul's statement: "The good I want to do, I fail to do; but what I do is the wrong against my will; and if what I do is against my will, clearly it is no longer I who am the agent, but sin that has its lodging in me" (Romans 7:19-20). This is a very explicit statement of the Christian teaching that man is by nature sinful and cannot perfect himself. I believe that our experience bears out the truth of this concept on every side.

Perhaps a much less evident proposition, yet one that carries the same character, is to be found in the Letter to the Hebrews. "When in former times God spoke to our forefathers, he spoke in fragmentary and varied fashion through the prophets. But in this final age he has spoken to us in the Son whom he has made heir to the whole universe" (Heb. 1:1-2). This is a very early Christological claim, which argues that in Jesus' life we have a fulfillment of all men's quest for the meaning of life and a normative revelation of God's will for us. It is a more tenuous statement than Paul's about the sinful nature of man, yet it also is a theological judgment based on experience. I believe that it is true on these grounds.

The oneness of God, the sinfulness of man, and the unique nature of Christ are all theological concepts to be found in the Bible. Along with many others we could cite, they purport to be statements of fact. The important thing is that the Christian claims they are *reasonable* propositions in the light of the evidence. This is quite different from simple points of view, although there is obvious overlapping. This is equally true of what is perhaps the most important kind of propositional narrative in the Bible, which I will discuss now.

Scripture as Disclosure Statements

It is my belief that the most important reason for studying the Bible is for its affect, its ability to awaken in us a sense of God's presence. Because of this it is best to hear the Scriptures read aloud, as we do in the liturgy. In this way the emotional impact of the narrative comes across most clearly. In earlier chapters I wrote about the feeling experienced in the symbolic and of the power of the poetic form. This was the "Aha!" experience, the sudden insight provoked by the magnetic attraction of the symbol or the discovery within the proposition. Our faith is awakened. Our love for God and our fellowmen is kindled. We discern the mystery of God within the proposition as a sudden discovery, and we are assured of God's presence in our world. I first discussed the nature of "disclosure" in the fourth chapter. It is perhaps a difficult notion to keep in mind, so if the reader is uncertain what I mean, it would be helpful for him to refer back to that section.

Disclosure is somewhat difficult to illustrate because such statements are very personal. What is the context of insights for one person is not for another. From the Old Testament there is, however, no more generally accepted example than the Twenty-third Psalm.

> The Lord is my shepherd; I shall want nothing.
>   He makes me lie down in green pastures,
> and leads me beside the waters of peace;
>   he renews life within me,
> and for his name's sake guides me in the right path.
> Even though I walk through a valley dark as death
> I fear no evil, for thou art with me,
>   thy staff and thy crook are my comfort.

The images on the surface are alien to technological, twentieth-century man. "Waters of peace," "staff," "crook," and "comfort" are, in a practical sense, meaningless. Yet I have seen persons ravaged by cancer, gasping for breath, find courage and strength to die in faith at the sound of these words.

The prophet Elijah is a favorite of mine. He was a man of great faith whose enthusiasm often got him into much trouble with King Ahab and his heathen wife, Jezebel. The story of Elijah's flight into the wilderness and his vision in the cave on Mt. Horeb is a constant source of meaning to me (see I Kings 19:1-21). I frequently hear God asking of me, "Why are you here, Elijah," even when I know very well that, as with the prophet, it was the Lord that brought me here in the first place.

We all know from the New Testament the power of the account of Jesus' nativity (Lk. 2:1-20), even though it is highly probable that the Evangelist incorporated into his Gospel a popular legend that had very little relation to "brute fact." But when we listen to the story read at Christmas this does not matter. It evokes in us a deep awareness of the mystery of God and of his Son, who came among us as a gift of pure love. The power of God-become-man, the Incarnation, is in this story. It opens the eyes of many to the wonder of it all.

The various accounts of Jesus' trial, death, and resurrection are also clear illustrations of a disclosure story. Compare the four narratives in as many Gospels and you will see there are factual discrepancies, but this is again beside the point. If we read and ponder the Passion, as it is called, one may well discover there the same faith that was seen in the Roman officer described as guarding the Cross. Of him Mark wrote: "And when the centurion who was standing opposite him [Jesus] saw how he died, he said,

'Truly this man was a son of God' " (Mk. 15:39). Or we can experience the revelation with the apostle Thomas, who doubted Jesus' resurrection. When indeed he saw the risen Christ, he could only cry in faith, "My Lord and my God" (Jn. 20:28).

The reading of the Holy Scriptures is rooted in its power to evoke in us a new disclosure of God's presence and to call us to faith. This is the heart of the Bible's function, if not its only purpose.

Summary

In this light it should be evident that arguments over the "literal truth" of Scripture are not only beside the point but destructive of the role of the Bible within Christian meaning. There are those who have made these sacred writings, not a *means* to know God and to give expression to their experience of him, but an *end* in themselves. Their faith stops with believing that these thirty-nine books of the Old Testament and twenty-seven books of the New Testament are a source of answers, an assurance of a kind that no man who believes himself to be human has a right to expect. The Bible has become an idol.

The main prevailing theme of this book is that our meaning of God is never the same as the experience of God, much less God himself. Fundamentalism of any kind— biblical, theological, liturgical—makes a finite world equivalent to an infinite god. Meaning is made up of symbol and sign, including myth and theological systems (as we shall see in the next chapter), which are very human efforts to give substance to an experience that is ultimately mysterious. This includes that meaning which we call the Bible! It is the product of the Church's experience within its environment and it must never be taken out of that context.

Yet it is a very special "product," which is normative in a number of ways for all other Christian meaning. It defines the Christian point of view. It possesses a kind of basic theological inquiry, which will give forceful movement to the later systematic explorations of human reason that lie ahead in the next chapter. Above all, it has a symbolic power second only to the person of our Lord himself. The Bible is *not* the Word of God; that is what Christ is. It is, in the mind of the Christian, the inspired record of that Word as nothing else. It is inspired because it is the product of the Christian community, in which we believe that the Holy Spirit works to lead us to the truth of God revealed in the Christ. That truth is not the simple one-for-one notion in which representations equal their referents but the truth that leads us into ultimate mystery.

This is to say that while I speak of the Bible as the "inspired record," one should not conclude from that expression that it is simply a testimony to *past* events in which God gives us special insight. The reading or hearing of the Holy Scriptures can be and should be a means of leading us into the *present* event of the Word of God. When I refer to the supreme value of the Bible as a means of disclosure it should be understood that these writings draw us to the knowledge of God in Christ, call us to faith, and hold us accountable before the Lord of all history.

Having said this, it is now necessary to move on to look at the Church's efforts to develop such a one-for-one truth, where the clear logic of human reason has sought to build understanding. I have written much about the importance of not reducing God to our propositions and not attempting to capture him in a literalism. There is a place, however, for the logic of reason, and this lies in the development of dogma and its systems.

REVIEW QUESTIONS

1. *What does it mean to say that the Bible is a creature of the Christian community and yet confronts, judges, and illuminates the life of the contemporary Christian community?*
2. *How many examples can the reader recall from the Bible which show the comparison between statements of points of view and statements of fact?*
3. *What is your favorite disclosure story from the Bible?*

chapter TEN

Dogma and systems

Finally, we arrive at what is technically understood to be theology: *conceptions or products of thinking that result from reflection upon the experience of God.* I wrote briefly about theology as part of the internal structure of religious meaning in the fourth chapter, when we were considering the nature of a sign and its use in propositions. Theology is, of course, the result of a very careful use of words as signs and the product of a logical and well-honed series of propositions. This is where the hard thinking comes; yet all that has gone before—experience, symbol, myth, Jesus, the Bible—must necessarily have preceded this discussion. In the chapter heading I have referred to the substance of Christian theology as "dogma" and "system." Those are not very popular words. Dogma calls up images of being dogmatic, a description of a *theological fundamentalism* in which the author of the dogma insists that he alone is right. Actually the word "dogma" comes from the Greek word for *thinking*, and refers in this chapter to a concept that is the product of our thought about the experience of God. "System" conjures up a stifling, closed arrangement of ideas, in which all new thought seems to be ruled out because the author of the system has described everything. It can also mean, however, an interrelated network of ideas or dogmas, and it is to this meaning that I refer here.

In discussing the Christian symbols and myths, focused in

the person of Jesus and enshrined in the Holy Scriptures, we have given most of our attention to the mysterious power of those images within our experience in which we *feel* the presence of God in Creation. We have seen the work of God within the history of the chosen people, culminating in the coming of the Christ, as the great biblical story. There has been much more emphasis upon the role of metaphor and inspired intuition, which engages us at the level of emotion, than upon the role of reason and concept. Now the emphasis must fall the other way. We must ask ourselves what all this means and answer as clearly and reasonably as possible.

There has always been a resistance to this kind of hard thinking. It can expose much foolishness, reveal our mistakes, and require us to retreat from some positions we have held in great emotional fervor. It is like the aging beauty who resists placing a bright light before her mirror that might reveal the sagging flesh, the wrinkles, and the discolored skin. Thinking, if not actually threatening, is not very exciting to some. It appears to make life a bit flat and dull—or so it would seem. It is something like a little child discovering that "there is no Santa Claus." Actually there is a Santa Claus, but we have to work through the whole process of thinking before we can recover the reality of a small child's wonder. Therefore, I would emphasize, particularly to those Christians who are filled with evangelical fervor and are suspicious of learning, that they must overcome their fear of hard thinking about their belief.

Thinking is necessary if we are not to become the victims of our feelings. I have said this before in Chapter Four, but it is worth repeating. The emotions are very fickle, as anyone who has loved knows. Thinking helps us get behind the feeling to the reason for it, and puts us in the larger picture. For example, someone comes to you and says, "My husband is inhuman. Every night he comes home from work and kicks the cat across the room." The thoughtful response to such inappropriate behavior is not, "Let's hope the cat learns to bite him back." Thinking might reveal that he kicks the cat because he cannot kick the boss at work and keep his job. Furthermore, we would have to see what goes on at work to understand why he wants to kick the boss. In this light, appropriate new action is more likely, and we avoid destructive behavior that only deepens the problem.

Christian dogma and systems have usually been the thoughtful response of the Church to behavior which was out of place for a member of Christ's Church. One early Christian sect, for example, cut off their sexual organs for God. The Church as a whole condemned this practice by countering the teaching behind it. The attempt is made to understand what error lies behind the action and to correct it by stating, *in terms of the thought forms of the time*, what is a balanced view of the depth and breadth of the Christian experience. The first great Christian theologian may have been Irenaeus (died about A.D. 200), who wrote a series of five books called *Against Heresies*. ("Heresy" comes from a word meaning "to choose" and is the term applied to what is judged to be erroneous or unbalanced thinking lying behind out-of-place Christian actions.) The heresy he opposed is called "gnosticism," which describes a group of people who separated themselves from other Christians because they claimed to have a special "knowledge" ("gnostic" comes from the Greek word "to know") which made them holier than anyone else. The gnostic heresy is always threatening the Church.

Irenaeus was good at dogma, but he did not give us a system. That was to come a thousand years later. He wrote as one schooled in the philosophy called Middle Platonism. A still greater theologian, Augustine of Hippo (354-430), wrote as a Neo-Platonist. Still later, Thomas Aquinas (c.

1225-1274), perhaps the author of the most significant Christian system, thought in the categories of Aristotle. Theologians today must employ the thought forms developed since the great German philosopher, Immanuel Kant (1724-1804): existentialism, process thought, transcendental Thomism, or perhaps linguistic analysis. I realize that all these names for philosophical schools mean nothing to most readers, but I think they are important to mention in passing for two reasons. First, they give labels to the change in dogma and systems that must take place as their philosophical foundation changes; and, second, if the reader wishes to pursue the subject beyond this chapter, he must begin to identify those schools of thought.

Amid this process of change within dogma and system, however, there is a consistent, unchanging *process of knowing* common to all periods of human history. This process of thinking may not always operate fully, efficiently, or consciously, but it is potentially in every one of us by virtue of our being human. The balance of this chapter will be devoted to a very brief summary of how this operates within the discipline of theology, using as illustrative material the Christian understanding of the Holy Spirit. My hope is that the reader can identify this process for himself and be able to work out his own religious meaning within a necessary, thoughtful rationale of what such a meaning is for him in terms of dogma (ideas), if not of system.

Is Something There?

If we are to know something, there has to be something there to be known. Knowing it, however, is not just a matter of looking at it out there, but of entering into a conversation with the phenomena of our experience in order to identify it. It begins in a process of "being with" or "meeting with" the possible something. Of course, we do not go to this meeting with an empty head, but we do need an open mind. In theological reflection we begin by looking at representative religious beliefs *without* injecting from the start our own personal commitment in a manner which does not allow for change.

In William Blatty's fascinating book, *The Exorcist*, the Jesuit priest, Fr. Karras, who is a trained psychiatrist, goes through a process of theological reflection. He begins by believing that an extremely demented twelve-year-old girl suffers from mental illness. He ends by identifying a demon. What "saved" him and the girl, in different ways, was his willingness to have an open mind. The priest started his treatment by testing the theory that what he experienced in the girl was one kind of "something" (mental illness), and ended up concluding that this did not fit the situation. It was, in fact, another "something" (a demon) no matter how unlikely this was in terms of contemporary presuppositions about reality.

The first thing we do in discovering if something is there is *research*. We ask what is the data of our experience? * In the New Testament there is an obvious awareness that the Spirit of God was present in the life of Jesus: his conception (Lk. 1:34), his baptism (Mk. 1:10), and the beginning of his ministry (Mk. 1:12; Lk. 4:14). The disciples believed that Jesus promised the gift of the Spirit after he left them (Jn. 16:7-11), probably in the light of an extraordinary experience of God's presence in their lives (Jn. 20:22; Acts 2:1-4 provide two accounts of such an experience). The early Church began to speak of the gifts of the Spirit (I Cor. 12:1-11), of which ecstatic speech was undoubtedly a part (I Cor. 14:1-6). In fact, Paul writes of God giving his Holy Spirit to men (I Thess. 4:8). All of this comes out

* "Data" is the collective name for what is perceived by our senses in experience.

of a Jewish heritage, where the Spirit of God was usually considered not a discrete thing but a term for speaking of God's presence in somebody in a particular form (Isaiah 11:2. But compare Wisd. of Sol. 6:12-25). All this is an example of what I mean by data.

Of course, there is the data of the experience of the Holy Spirit throughout the history of Christianity, including today, but I have chosen to limit this discussion for the sake of brevity to the Scriptures.

Second, research leads to the subtle art of *interpretation*. (Some readers may be familiar with *hermeneutics*, which is the same thing.) Interpretation runs through the entire theological process, but it may conveniently be isolated at this point.

If one has ever had his eyes examined by an optometrist or ophthalmologist, he will recall that at one point in the examination the doctor tests to see what lenses help the patient see best. He tries first one and then another, saying, "Which is better, this one or that one?" He works on the basis of a highly educated guess or an informed intuition as an optometrist. It is, so to speak, to look at the data and say, "Maybe this is the 'something' there. Let's see if it works."

In a similar manner, looking at the experience of the Spirit of God in the fourth century, the Church asked itself, "What if the Holy Spirit were, in fact, a person of God, of the same nature and just like the Father or the Son. Let's see if it works." This was an *insight*, an intuitive guess, a product of the Church's imagination, rooted in both the Jewish tradition and current philosophical trends, but different from both. The Jews believed that God was completely one, and to speak of his Spirit was simply a way of referring to his presence. The current philosophy of that day did not attribute personhood to God in any form. The important thing to see here is that the Church was imagining, with the signs available to it from the past and in the

contemporary environment, to see if it could draw together a balanced concept that fit its experience. It was
searching for the "lens" which would enable it to see best.

In the third place, interpretation demands that we look at
history (refer back to Chapter Eight). We cannot discuss
here the many problems associated with the study of history, but need only note that the theologian draws heavily
upon man's previous understanding of his experience and
what he has judged to be true to see if something is there.
This is not because he is a slave to the past, but because he
believes that the consistency of God's purpose requires that
what is explicit in the present needs to be seen as implicit in
the past. Furthermore, if we understand what we inherit
from the past we are better able to understand the present.

There was a tradition that the Church did *not* affirm:
that the Holy Spirit represents the feminine dimension of
the Godhead. It is not without significance that the cult of
the Virgin Mary, the Mother of Jesus, grew in importance
in the mainstream of Christianity after the fifth century,
which also gave expression to a divine femininity, while the
Holy Spirit received much less attention. One wonders
whether the classical dogma of the Holy Spirit was adequate to the ongoing experience of God's presence among
us, since this other thinking meaning of the cult of the
Blessed Virgin seemed more effective in expressing the
abiding presence of God's love.

What I am offering is nothing more than an illustration
of how a particular *interpretation* can be questioned in the
light of the analysis of subsequent history. This brings us,
fourth, face-to-face with the issue of whether this or alternative notions of the divine presence in the world is an
adequate expression of the experience. This is the *dialectic*
process. The purpose of dialectic is to expose the basic
conflict in outlook among reasoning theologians. In doing
this it also acknowledges the limits of man's understanding

and reveals in what ways different persons are conditioned by different limits.

The classical Christian dogma of the Holy Spirit, derived in the fourth and fifth centuries, is the result of a post-ecstatic intellectualist tradition, using Neo-Platonic categories. The Christian experience had become more or less institutionalized in the Sacraments, the monastic communities, and in long rhetorical sermons. "Institutionalization," please note, is not necessarily either good or bad; it just always happens. To think is human, and thinking in this age was done abstractly, removed from the concrete data, by playing with the relationship of numbers.

This was a different world from that of most of the Bible, where the experience of the Spirit was conceived in concrete terms as the power of God in creation ("A mighty wind [spirit] that swept over the surface of the waters," Genesis 1:2), the breath of man (God "breathed into his nostrils the breath of life," Genesis 2:7), or as the invisible power that moves among us ("The wind blows where it wills; you hear the sound of it, but you do not know where it comes from," Jn. 3:8.) It is also a very different world from that of the Christian mystic, who knew the Spirit in ecstatic experience.

Today we tend to think in very personal terms. There is a long history, beginning with Augustine of Hippo, of drawing an analogy between the Holy Spirit and love. For Augustine it was a fairly abstract love, for us today probably less so. For example, Paul Tillich, a theologian of the post-World War II generation, spoke of the divine presence as the faith and love of the Christian community. Daniel Day Williams, a contemporary process theologian, describes the coming together of love, which we know from others, and he identifies with the Spirit and reason that is traditionally identified with Christ. These two forces, he says, draw us into a oneness with the Father.

It is important that one see that four notions of the Holy Spirit have been mentioned: the biblical or impersonal divine power within Creation; the classical or the third person of the Trinity; the ecstatic or dramatic evidence of God's presence within persons; and the ideas of the Spirit as the love between persons. Perhaps the Holy Spirit is all four, any combination of the four, or more. The point is that the dialectic pattern is clear, which we need to understand in this process of the theological knowing. We compare, we contrast, and we hope to arrive at a higher synthesis.

The Middle Term: Conversion

Some scholars say that theology needs to be carried on without commitment to a religious faith. Up to this point it is possible. Human reason can examine the possible options for interpreting the data, in the light of historical and dialectical investigation, without passing any particular judgment. Yet Christian dogma and systems in theology purport to tell us something revealed by God, and do not end with human reason. This demands faith, which assumes that God illumines our reason. This illumination is more than what we find in the Bible. It is a faith that operates within a living community. Yet that community itself, as we have seen in Chapter Seven, is in process.

The process involves the coalition of the Church's human history with the presence of God, calling us into deeper understanding. In other words it is a community *in* the world but not *of* the world (I Jn. 4:1-6). It is the experience itself of the Holy Spirit in some form—power, person of God, ecstasy, love—leading us into the truth, as the Church believes Jesus has promised (Jn. 15:26-27). The divine presence inspires our thoughtful understanding.

There is no way to argue ourselves to the presence of God. The need for God's initiation of such faith has always been implicit in the Church's approach to theological truth. We are raised, we do not raise ourselves, from a level of knowing that is our doing to one that is God's (see II Cor. 12:2). Such knowledge is ultimately inexpressible, and when it is given expression, it is still conditioned by our history and community. Yet it carries a conviction that possesses a vertical dimension. It looks outside the world. Understanding is not to carry around a photographic image of the external world but to see as God sees. We know, not for the satisfaction of knowledge but to possess values that are God's. We have fallen in love with that which transcends ourselves.

This is conversion. It is a gift, which is necessary before entering into the following discussion of theological reflection. Such reflection has as its purpose, not just to determine what might be the possibilities of "something" being there, but to come to a conclusion of *what* that something is, to say *what* is true.

What is There?

There were four dimensions of theological reflection—research, interpretation, history, and dialectic—discussed under the heading of being with and sharing with the possible "something." This was a free, possibly uncommitted, act of the imagination. It was a testing of the possibilities, some of which could be highly improbable, as was illustrated in the example of Fr. Karras in the novel, *The Exorcist.* Yet just as the priest in the book came to a personal commitment, growing out of a conversion, there comes a point when we make a decision on the basis of *what* we believe to be true.

The difference can be illustrated this way. Debating teams in high school and college are often made up of persons who are skilled in taking either side of an issue, based simply on the chance of a draw. For example, I would personally have no difficulty arguing either side of private versus public education. I have been happily involved in both. There are issues, however, about which I have made a decision, and those I cannot debate on both sides. For example, I have a commitment on abortion-on-demand because of my belief as to God's gift of life. Where we have made a decision of belief, we move beyond the first four functional categories and we understand our experience in the light of our belief.

This understanding is *not* a matter of imposing answers upon experience but of *discovering* the implications of our personal stance in our experience. It is a process of discovering, not an argument from a set of already formulated answers. This is what is meant by *foundations*. The very term "foundations" implies that we root our belief in *what* God is to his world in the ground of our everyday experience. Foundations seek to answer the question of what may be the rock of our experience upon which may be laid that reality in which all things ultimately are resolved in God. It is a fifth issue on the way to dogma and systems.

I realize that the understanding of foundations is difficult to grasp. The reader needs to review what was said in the first chapter about the nature of meaning. Remember that what we see as "real" is what the meaning we build allows us to see, and our meaning is always a *selection* from experience in terms of a certain predisposition of mind. If we have been moved by the love of God, which is the initial act of conversion, to a predisposition of faith, then we will build our meaning in terms of God's presence in our experience. We will seek to live by God's values, and *we will expect to perceive in our experience reasons for concluding what God is*. This is to say that reason will be for us a way of understanding what God is, but only in terms of our faith.

To return to the illustration of the meaning of the Holy Spirit, this understanding is based on a faith commitment that the divine can reasonably be expected to be present in our world working out God's purpose. In this fifth category of foundations we ask ourselves how is that true and what does it tell us about God as Holy Spirit. My argument would be that I see the greatest sense of divine working to the good of all things in the presence of love. I do not deny that this love can work through ecstatic experience, but it seems to be most clearly present in the ordinary lives of people in community who are supporting each other in fulfilling that which is most satisfying and fulfilling to them. It is not a coercive presence, forcing itself on us. It appears to me that where people are forced into certain patterns of life their humanity is not fulfilled but destroyed. Rather, the divine presence is God *inviting* us into a fuller life. I find this true in my family, among my friends, and in the Church. I sense it in the natural world about me. All of this seems true in spite of the obvious failure and sin that surrounds us.

This is then an exercise in the foundations of the divine presence in experience. Sixth, it is very easy to move almost without knowing it, to *dogma*. Remember that dogma is an idea, which is the result of thinking. The idea of the Holy Spirit that is derived from the previous category within the context of research, interpretation, history, and dialectic, is this: the Holy Spirit is the power of God continually working in personal ways in his world to see that his purpose may indeed be fulfilled. We do not know what that purpose is except that it is found in a oneness with God. The Holy Spirit is given to us in the Church in a special way, not in any one kind of form and yet working throughout creation. The Holy Spirit is love-making-whole.

This is not to deny that the Holy Spirit is the third Person of the Holy Trinity, of the same nature as the Father and the Son, and proceeding from the Father through the Son—or together from both Father and Son, which is the classical dogma from the fifth century. The Holy Spirit as love-making-whole does give a more contemporary value to "person," avoids the issue of what "nature" may mean and how we know it, and rephrases the notion of "procession" in terms of our experience. My contention is that theology must constantly engage in this kind of reappraisal of its propositions.

We have asked ourselves *what* is there and we inevitably come, as a seventh item, to *systems*. A system is an answer to the question of what this dogma has to do with what else we believe about God and man. The "whatness" here is the big question of how it all fits together into some kind of overarching picture of the whole world under God. Systems are not very popular these days, although a few theologians have tried them. I suspect all of us have unexpressed systems, which we need to clarify if for no other reason than to discover their defects.

Perhaps it can be seen that the dogma of the Holy Spirit has immediate implications for several other theological ideas. I spoke of the relationship of God's presence to the Church, and there is, therefore, the dogma of the Church to consider. I have not mentioned the sacraments specifically, such as Baptism and the Eucharist, but these are also obviously involved. In another direction, Jesus as the Word or reason of God joins with the Holy Spirit as the love of God and, therefore, it is important to understand the relationship between Christ present among us and the Holy Spirit. It is possible to build in this manner continuously.

but I would hope that the reader understands by now what I mean by system and the fact that systems, more than any other category in theological reflection, are open to question and change.

Summary

This has been a long and probably difficult chapter. The next and concluding chapter will necessarily continue in this same vein. It will, however, speak to the whole matter of this book, whereas at this point I am concerned that the reader understand the progression we have made in considering the specific substance of the Christian meaning of God. We started with the event of the Christian faith, the presence of Jesus of Nazareth, who is for us the primal symbol of God. His life, death, and resurrection fulfill the most profound myths of man's understanding of life under God. Although he is also a sign to us, this only follows upon his symbolic and mythic power. We then turned to the Bible, which also carries a symbolic meaning but is more of a normative source of signative (in the form of signs) meaning. Finally we came to theological dogma and systems, which have little symbolic force at all but seek to satisfy the need for propositions that clarify and share our meaning of God in a way that frees us from pure emotion and gives us a basis for reasoned Christian behavior.

That move from Jesus through the Bible to dogma and systems, and beyond to action, inevitably faces us with the testing of the truth of our meaning. If we are to act upon what we believe to be true, that action will inevitably produce conflict and challenge. Therefore, we are faced with the responsibility of constantly testing the validity of what we believe to be the meaning of our experience of God. This brings us to the last and necessary chapter.

REVIEW QUESTIONS

1. *What is the principal value in the process of developing dogma and systematic religious meaning?*
2. *What is the process of discovering whether or not "something is there," and does this require a specific commitment to "something" before it is done?*
3. *What is the relationship between conversion, dogma, and system?*

Part V

THE TRUTH
OF MEANING

chapter ELEVEN

Is it true?

We started this book by distinguishing between experience and meaning. Meaning is what we make of our experience. It is, we hope, always expanding, and yet it never can comprehend all of our experience—unless we are God. The experience of God is the experience of the infinite, and the meaning of finite persons like you and me is necessarily always finite, limited. To ask if something is "true" is to inquire whether or not our *meaning* correctly reflects our experience or, to put it another way, what is happening to us. Therefore, since truth as we know it always relates to meaning, not experience, we never have the whole truth. Only God has that.

Jesus, when he was being tried before Pontius Pilate, the Roman governor in Jerusalem, responded to Pilate's question as to whether he was a king by saying, "My task is to bear witness to the truth." Pilate's response to that was, "What is truth?" (Jn. 18:38). The irony of this passage is that the Fourth Evangelist apparently intends us to understand that the "truth" was there in person before Pilate, and yet the Roman governor could not grasp it. To the evangelist, Jesus is the Word, the truth that is God become man (Jn. 1:14). We are all in a sense like Pilate. We can never completely become one with the truth until we are fully one "in Christ." As Paul says, "Now we see only puzzling reflections in a mirror, but then we shall see face to face" (I Cor. 13:12).

The Greek word for truth helps us see this point further. It is made up of the word for "forgetfulness," with a prefix attached that means "un." The reasoning behind this is that the person, in the process of being born, *forgets* what he knew in the presence of God. (Some Greek thinkers taught that the soul was eternal and birth was a process of being separated from the presence of the divine.) Acquiring the truth was, then, a matter of "un-forgetting" or remembering what the soul had known when it was with God. We all know the problem of remembering, and that we can never completely recapture the past.

How do we judge, however, whether our meaning is true or not? That is the basic question for this chapter. It brings us right back to where we began this book, with experience. *The truth of our meaning is determined by comparing that meaning against our experience.* We test it over and over again. We need to remember, however, that this meaning is made up of four elements: feeling, common sense, intuition, and thinking. "Testing" requires that we get a certain distance on the relationship of those things we want to compare, and that we do not become so emotionally involved that we cannot "see the forest for the trees." As I have said in the fourth chapter, thinking is the dimension of meaning that gives us this distance.

Let me illustrate this point. All of us have come into a group of people for the first time and had the *feeling* that they did not like us. Perhaps a couple whisper to one another, and our intuition *suggests* that they are talking about us. After all, does not *common sense* tell us that when someone whispers it is because they are saying something they do not want others to hear? Do we know, however, that our feelings, intuition, and common-sense judgment are true? The only way to answer that is to *think* about what is happening when you come into the group. It may be that you feel uncomfortable in a new group for reasons that lie buried in your past and have nothing to do with this present group. It is entirely possible that the whispering couple were talking about plans for tomorrow and that both of them, as unlikely as it may seem, are suffering from laryngitis.

Thinking—which requires a reasoned, logical analysis of what is happening on the basis of all the available data, and drawing together the most *reasonable* statement that describes and/or explains it all—is essential to making a judgment as to truth. We live in a society that is suspicious of too much thinking. Americans are high on feeling and common sense and are very critical of intellectuals. It is popular among some people in theological education to say, "I don't care what you think, what really matters is what you feel." That statement in itself, however, is a thinking meaning. Expressing our reason for caring about feelings rather than thoughts is itself a thought, which may or may not be true. We cannot escape thinking, and it is best that we do it consciously and well rather than delude ourselves into thinking that thinking is unimportant. No human can talk without reasoning and thinking, although we often do it very poorly.

One of the most distinguished American Anglican theologians was William Porcher DuBose (1836-1918), my distant predecessor as Dean of the School of Theology of the University of the South. DuBose once wrote, "Right reason is to know God as the eternal reason, meaning, and purpose of all things." The Fourth Evangelist said of Jesus, the Word of God, that he is the truth, the express image of God (Jn. 1:17; 8:32; 14:6). I would add that truth ultimately can be judged only by reason. Our concern in this chapter, therefore, is for right reason, that we might know the truth as a means of knowing God.

To Judge the Truth

How do we go about judging what is true? I have already suggested that it is the result of *testing* our conceptual statement of what we believe to be true against the data of our experience. For example, if I say that the moon is made of green cheese, it is possible for me to hold that theory as long as what we see of the moon and (now that man has traveled there) what we taste, touch, hear, and smell of the moon does not contradict or falsify this concept.

In other words, a statement is true if it *best explains* all the available data of our experience. Many concepts are not as easily proven true or false as the one about the moon and green cheese. We often have to judge between several attempts to describe and/or explain the data of our experience, of which perhaps the debate over the wave or particle theories as to the nature of light are an often cited example. (There are reasons for holding one or the other.) The act of judging the best concept involves certain principles as to the way we go about arriving at a judgment. There are six such principles we need to keep in mind.

First of all, there is the act of selecting the data to be described. This is always an unconscious process in part—we are not aware of most of our experience—and it can also be a conscious process in part. For example, a person can say that he is only going to look at data that has to do with physical cause (the fire that makes the water boil), and, therefore, data that might lead to God as a cause will be excluded. We must be aware of the fact of selection and our particular "filters" for screening data. They are always arbitrary and often exist for unconscious reasons.

Second, and on the other side of selection, a person must be open to the new data that the very act of testing his concept will generate. Penicillin, which has saved the lives of countless thousands of people, was discovered by Alexander Fleming after a mold had accidently contaminated a bacterial culture in which he was testing something very different. As another example of the same thing, there is at present a great new interest in transcendental meditation, partly as a result of certain data that psychologists unexpectedly turned up in examining patterns of human behavior.

We also need to acknowledge, in the third place, that the judgment of truth assumes that there is an intelligibility to life. Things follow one another logically. There is a reason for things being as they are. For example, if I see a vision—as some friends of mine say they have—there is a reason for it. It may be that I have consumed an hallucinogenic drug such as LSD, or that I am suffering from brain damage, or that God is speaking to me. Things do *not* "just happen."

Fourth, we judge to be true (the true reason for the data we have selected and have been willing to acknowledge even after selection) only that which is capable of being verified. We cannot say something is true just because we feel it is or, much worse, because we want it to be true. Obviously, we experience data within ourselves, but the judgment of truth also requires that we relate the data so experienced to another who is independent of ourselves. This is simply another way of saying that we need to have a distance on what we are judging in order to keep the subjective element at a minimum. My mother told me about God when I was very young, and at the age of twenty-five I had an ecstatic experience in which I sensed a new consciousness. In relating the two—the God-my-mother-told-me-about and the ecstasy—I am making a judgment that is independent of myself. If I claim that the ecstasy was an experience of the God-my-mother-told-me-about, it is because it is the *simplest* (the statistically most probable) correlation available to me. There are no easier explanations:

such as I took LSD thirty minutes before the ecstasy; or the fact that many people *naturally* have emotional highs (which the psychologist Abraham Maslow called "peak experiences").

Not only must our explanation be the simplest possible, but, fifth, it also needs to be as complete as possible. Any conceptual analysis attempting to be true must seek to account for all of the data. Langdon Gilkey, a theologian at the University of Chicago, wrote a book several years ago called *Naming the Whirlwind*, in which he argued that those who say we cannot speak meaningfully of God ignore some of the admitted data of their experience. If we say, he insists, that "God is dead" we are giving an incomplete analysis of the data of our life and therefore we are being untruthful. We are not, Gilkey said, taking into account man's feeling of being grounded or rooted in something unconditioned; our sense of limits implies the unlimited beyond, our investment in values, and the persistent mystery in life. (I realize that the reader may not understand the four categories in this last sentence. I list them only for the sake of making the example specific and concrete; and if the intended meaning is not apparent, this does not prevent grasping the basic idea.)

Finally, judgment of truth involves a commitment to a quest, because there is always going to be unexplained experience in our conceptual analysis. Truth is dynamic and expansive! We believe that in the act of judging we are always expanding the horizons of our knowing and there is always more to be known (unless we are God). The act of knowing, including judging, is something like assembling the "nest of boxes" some of us may recall from our early childhood or from the childhood of our own offspring. We start with the smallest box and put it into a slightly larger one. Then we fit those into a still larger one, and the three then are put in a larger one than that. The process can go forever. Each box represents an horizon and each horizon includes what we knew in the last one and still more.

A specific illustration from the Judaeo-Christian tradition might be this one. The Hebrews knew the Law of Moses, which is generally summed up in the Ten Commandments. This is a little box. Then came Jesus, the fulfillment of the Law, who expanded our understanding of what the Law meant. This is a slightly larger box. The whole ethical system of the Middle Ages, out of which developed the theory of natural law, was an attempt to give Jesus as the fulfillment a still larger "box." Now in the twentieth century we are debating the whole question of ethics and law in terms of their context or environment, and this is an even bigger box. I am sure that still greater boxes or wider horizons await future generations. The question of truth is open-ended.

The Subjective Nature of Truth

Truth is not something, however, that is waiting for us "out there," outside of ourselves. What we judge to be real is what we judge to be true, and as I have said for the nature of reality I say now for truth itself. It is the *product* of the *self's interaction with the data of his senses:* what he sees, hears, smells, touches, and tastes in his experience. The data is, to repeat myself, selected by the self. Therefore, truth is always subjective, always related to the self. It is always a result of the self's interpretation.

There are a number of factors which influence the self—you or me—in making that selection. There are the unconscious forces in each of us that color how we see things. Sometimes we explain why we think the way we do by saying, "I just can't help it. It's how I see it." This is an effort to express a condition of perception deeply rooted in our unconscious feelings. Then there is the individual's bias, determined by his own self-interest. (I was once explaining to a rather conservative fellow priest how well attended an evening Eucharist was in my parish, to which he replied, "Don't confuse my prejudice against evening Eucharists with the facts!") Third, there is the bias created by our upbringing. As a Southerner living for some years in the Midwest, I discovered it was very hard for me to overcome the Midwestern stereotype of me as a lazy bigot reared on a plantation. Finally, to err is human. None of us is unconditioned by the fallibility of the human mind.

This does not excuse us, however. If there is, as I have said, a necessary intelligibility to experience, then it is our task to enable reason to prevail wherever and whenever it can in the cause of truth. To experience God's presence—another way of speaking of the grace of God—is not just to feel the presence of the mysterious, but to know God, as DuBose said, as "right reason." This requires a constant attentiveness to those conditions that influence our judgment and a willingness to examine the data and let reason prevail. One important way of doing this is to enter into conversation with other truth-seekers.

The Church in the last century generally believed that the story of Adam and Eve was an account of how man was created—as if we had been there taking movies. The history of mankind was thought to be about six thousand years. Along came Charles Darwin and his book, *The Origin of the Species*, which made the theory of evolution current, and since then the Church has had to face the reasonable conclusion that the earth is billions of years old and that man, having evolved from more primitive species, is about one to two million years old. This is what is known as the self-correcting process of learning, and is what happens—"in fits and starts"—whenever man thinks reasonably.

"The shoe can fit on the other foot." In the fifties it was argued that it is meaningless to speak of God because there are no conditions under which we can falsify his existence or show it as untrue. An English philosopher, Antony Flew, illustrated this from the now well-known parable of the invisible gardener. Two explorers in the jungle, as the story goes, come across an open place where flowers are growing. One says, "There must be a gardener here." The other replies, "I'm doubtful. Let's see." So they build a barbed-wire, electric fence around it, patrol it with blood-hounds, and stand watch. No gardener appears. The believer insists, "I am sure there is a gardener. How else do you explain the flowers? Surely he is one who can pass through electrified barbed-wire, cannot be smelled by bloodhounds, and is invisible to us." The skeptic answers, "How can we tell, if you disallow all means by which we can discover whether or not there is a gardener?" The answer is intended to be, of course, that to speak of the gardener (or God) when there are no criteria to prove he does not exist is to refer to what is meaningless.

The reply to this parable has been stated in several ways. The simplest is this. No one says that God is an *object* of our experience, which the parable presumes in all talk of fences, dogs, and watch-keeping. God is only known *through* objects, such as symbols and myths, by those who have faith. For the faithful, however, there are criteria of falsification or verification in terms of God's meaning to them. It is a matter of one's subjective commitment and subsequent judgment. In other words, what kind of data will we acknowledge? There are faithful Jews today who question what God might be because the God they served in the past would not have allowed the murder of six million Jews by Hitler in World War II. The whole question of the truth of God, Christ, and his Church is very much dependent upon the faith of the self or subject—you or me —and how that is worked out in our personal experience.

Pluralism and Dialogue

John Allegro, an English scholar, recently wrote a book entitled *The Sacred Mushroom and the Cross*, in which he says that the New Testament is filled with problems of interpretation, but that he has found the key to solve them all. By a very subtle and complex study of words in the New Testament he demonstrates that Christianity is essentially a fertility cult, in which the hallucinogenic mushroom, *Amanitia muscaria*, has a central function. For example, the opening words of the Lord's Prayer in Aramaic (Jesus' native tongue), Allegro argues, is really a reference to the Sumerian phrase for this sacred mushroom, and that early Christians knew this and were actually involving the power of the mushroom in the Lord's Prayer to which Jesus had introduced them.

This is a serious scholarly work. I cite it because it probably seems utterly fantastic to the reader and because it illustrates the point that different people can come up with various versions of the truth from the same experience—in this case, reading the New Testament. There is no way for us to be absolutely positive Allegro is wrong and we are right. This is an indication of the fact that until we know the world as God knows it, there will be always multiple truths or realities. This is what I mean by "pluralism." Our unconscious past, our individual needs, our training, and our sheer humanity lead us all to build meaning that differs one from another. Each meaning, given these presuppositions derived from our unconscious past, individual needs, training, and sheer humanity, can have a certain reasonableness.

It happens that Allegro's argument is not very good because it is neither the simplest nor the most complete explanation of the data in the New Testament. It is mostly fanciful, although fun to follow. Because it is so "far out" it is very difficult to compare it with other points of view. Generally speaking, however, a greater approximation of truth does come when multiple truths enter into dialogue with one another. It is quite possible to be open to the truth of another without surrendering the truth we hold but instead enriching our meaning or even arriving at a higher level of truth.

For example, the world into which our Lord came was largely a Jewish one, operating out of a particular kind of world view. It soon came into contact with the Greek world, with a very different bias. Although some would question this, I think it can be safely said that the Greek approach greatly enriched the Jewish. Today we are seeing a great interest in Far Eastern religious thought. Some fear that Christians who study Buddhist and Hindu world views will "lose their faith" or deny the uniqueness of Christ. My own conviction is that, as with the Greek, such a cross-fertilization of thought can only draw us closer to the ultimate truth that Jesus came to show us in God.

No meaning, tested reasonably against our experience, can in the final analysis lead us away from God, who is reason. We can be deluded and fall away, which is why we need to examine our thoughts against those of our collaborative community, the Church. It is to this delusion that the author of Ephesians referred in warning his readers against being "tossed by the waves and whirled about by every fresh gust of teaching" (Eph. 4:14). As I suggested in the fourth chapter, the wider the collaboration the more likely we are to be right. The general process of searching reason, however, is God's grace in one direction: the fulfillment of that which Christ came to reveal and to make real in our lives (Col. 1:9-3:17).

Summary

We come to the end. What I have sought to show the reader is that to speak of God is to enter into a *hopeful process* in which all mankind, in general, and the Christian community in particular, has been engaged throughout time or, at least for the last two thousand years. Our experience of God has persisted. Man is, without question, unceasingly involved in the sacred, whether he is willing to affirm it or not. In times like our own many have become particularly conscious of this experience.

My advice, even warning, throughout has been to distinguish between that experience and the meaning we make of it. The meaning takes a number of forms—feeling, common sense, intuition, and thinking—and each form has its strength and its dangers. It is important that we seek a balance of all four forms. Nothing in such meaning can rightly be identified with the mind of God, and even the most holy tradition needs to be held with humility. Tradition is not the same as God. If we do anything more we make idols of our symbols and myths, our dogmas and systems, and this only obscures the God who seeks to speak through them to us.

If we understand, however, the nature of religious meaning, it may become for us a most valuable instrument in holding fast to the Gospel, the good news that God loves us and cares for us. In worship and prayer, in reading and meditation, in study and discourse, the call of God can be heard in power and clarity, in a way that can be shared with others, and offer the hope for the future and for the maturity in Christ that God promised.

REVIEW QUESTIONS

1. *What is truth as it relates to us? to God?*
2. *What are the six items involved in the judgment of truth and how do these relate to the subjective nature of truth?*
3. *Why in pluralistic culture is dialogue important in the understanding of truth?*